LONG BEARD

Hans Langseth, from Norway, is buried in Kensett, Iowa—well, most of him is. His 17-foot, 6-inch beard, which is considered the longest in the world, is proudly displayed in the Smithsonian. For more cool facts, read on!

Louise Rozett, Editor
Allicette Torres, Art Director
The Design Lab, Book Design

Library of Congress Cataloging-in-Publication Data
Fast facts about the 50 states.
    p. cm. — (America the beautiful, third series)
  Includes index.
  ISBN 978-0-531-24700-6; 0-531-24700-7
  1. U.S. states—Miscellanea—Juvenile literature. 2. United States—Miscellanea—Juvenile
literature. I. Title: Fast facts about the fifty states. II. Series.
  E180.F37 2009
  973–dc22   2009002048

1 2 3 4 5 6 7 8 9 10 R 16 15 14 13 12 11 10

FAST FACTS ABOUT THE 50 STATES

PLUS **PUERTO RICO** AND **WASHINGTON, D.C.**

Children's Press®
An Imprint of Scholastic Inc.
New York ★ Toronto ★ London ★ Auckland ★ Sydney
Mexico City ★ New Delhi ★ Hong Kong
Danbury, Connecticut

THINGS YOU
ABOUT YOUR

The following is a partial list of things YOU should know about your country:

★ **Superman lives in Illinois.**

★ **Burros in Arizona celebrate the 4th of July by eating eggs that fry on the sizzling streets.**

★ **If you love green Jell-O, you should live in Utah; if you love chocolate Kisses or soft pretzels, you should live in Pennsylvania.**

★ **The Etch A Sketch was born in Ohio.**

SHOULD KNOW COUNTRY

So how do we know all this?

Here's how: We held a contest, asking a bunch of Super Smarties (aka librarians) to tell us the coolest, wackiest, and wildest facts about their states. Before we knew it, hundreds of librarians from coast to coast had sent us AMAZING facts about their states.

After a lot of teeth gnashing and hair pulling (hey, it was hard!), we picked ten—and ONLY ten—incredible facts about each state from all the entries. You are now holding the result in your hands!

Read on and enjoy, trivia and history fans!

TRUTH – JUSTICE – THE AMERICAN WAY

CONTENTS

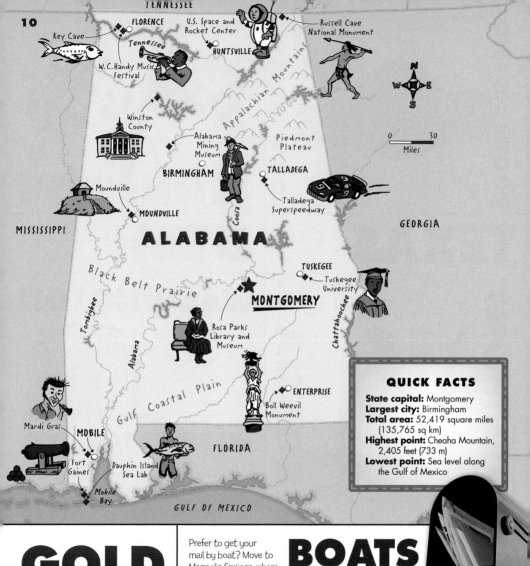

TENNESSEE

Key Cave

FLORENCE

U.S. Space and
Rocket Center

Russell Cave
National Monument

Tennessee

W. C. Handy Music
Festival

HUNTSVILLE

Appalachian Mountains

Winston
County

Alabama
Mining
Museum

Piedmont
Plateau

BIRMINGHAM

TALLADEGA

Moundville

Talladega
Superspeedway

MOUNDVILLE

GEORGIA

MISSISSIPPI

Coosa

ALABAMA

Black Belt Prairie

TUSKEGEE

Tuskegee
University

Tombigbee

Alabama

MONTGOMERY

Chattahoochee

Rosa Parks
Library and
Museum

Gulf Coastal Plain

ENTERPRISE

Boll Weevil
Monument

QUICK FACTS

State capital: Montgomery
Largest city: Birmingham
Total area: 52,419 square miles
   (135,765 sq km)
Highest point: Cheaha Mountain,
   2,405 feet (733 m)
Lowest point: Sea level along
   the Gulf of Mexico

Mardi Gras

MOBILE

FLORIDA

Fort
Gaines

Dauphin Island
Sea Lab

Mobile
Bay

GULF OF MEXICO

GOLD IN THE COLD

In February 2002, Birmingham-born bobsledder Vonetta Flowers became the first person from Alabama—and the first person of African descent—to win gold in a Winter Olympics.

Prefer to get your mail by boat? Move to Magnolia Springs, where the Magnolia River is home to the only all-water mail delivery system in the continental United States!

BOATS AND NOTES

ROCKET MAN

At NASA's Marshall Space Flight Center in Huntsville, German scientist Wernher von Braun developed the rockets that sent American astronauts to the moon in 1969! How's that for flying high?

ROSA ROCKS

When civil rights activist Rosa Parks refused a bus driver's order to give up her seat to a white man in Montgomery in 1955, she ignited the civil rights movement and rocked America. Thanks, Rosa!

HANKIE SONGS

Need a good cry? Just listen to some Hank Williams! The legendary crooner from Alabama is famous for tearjerkers like "Your Cheatin' Heart" and "I'm So Lonesome I Could Cry."

THE BIG SIT

The country's largest office chair stands a proud 31-feet tall in Anniston. It's made of 10 tons of steel and can withstand winds up to 85 miles per hour!

IT'S OUTTA HERE!

Despite racist hate mail and death threats, Mobile's Hank Aaron shattered Babe Ruth's homerun record when he knocked his 715th homer out of the park on April 8, 1974.

GOING FOR THE GOLD

At the 1936 Olympic games, African American athlete Jesse Owens won four gold medals. He was not honored by an American president until 1955.

HEADS UP!

In 1954, Ann Hodges was just minding her own business on her couch in Oak Grove when an 8.5 pound meteorite smashed through her roof and landed on her! Ouch!

HELP!

On February 16, 1968, the first 911 call was made in Haleyville. The bright red phone that received that first call is now retired and living in a Haleyville museum.

ALABAMA

THE YELLOWHAMMER STATE

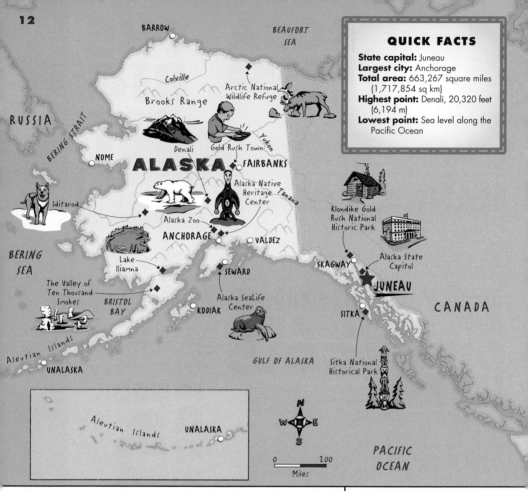

QUICK FACTS

State capital: Juneau
Largest city: Anchorage
Total area: 663,267 square miles
(1,717,854 sq km)
Highest point: Denali, 20,320 feet
(6,194 m)
Lowest point: Sea level along the
Pacific Ocean

SUPERSIZED STATE

Alaska is one big state! In fact, you could fit 1/5th of the combined "Lower 48" states inside its borders. (But it's probably better for everyone if you don't!)

HUNGRY HUNTERS

Hungry in Alaska? Go fish! Alaskans are allowed to hunt more fish and game than residents in other states because grocery stores are super scarce.

The Iditarod is a musher's marathon. The course is 1,150 freezing-cold miles from Anchorage to Nome, and it took the current record holder nearly ten days to finish! BRRRR!

MUSHING MARATHON

OIL ON THE MOVE

The Trans-Alaska Pipeline is 800 miles long, 48 inches in diameter, and has been moving oil through three mountain ranges and under 800 rivers and streams since 1977. That's some pipe!

MIDNIGHT SUN

In Barrow, Alaska, the sun stays up for 24 hours on the first day of summer. And on the first day of winter, it doesn't bother to rise at all!

SHAKING AND QUAKING

The most powerful earthquake recorded in North America occurred in Anchorage on Good Friday in 1964. Effects of the quake were observed as far away as Louisiana and South Africa!

WHAT'S FOR DESSERT?!

If you're not a Native Alaskan, Eskimo Ice Cream might scare you. Its ingredients can include fish liver, reindeer fat, and seal oil. Hey—don't knock it until you try it!

DEAR SANTA...

Ever mailed a letter to Santa? It probably ended up in North Pole, Alaska. The town receives—and answers!—mail from all over the world for the jolly fellow.

EAST MEETS WEST

Both the easternmost and westernmost points of the United States are in Alaska. How can that be? Alaska straddles the 180th Meridian, the global dividing line between all eastern and western longitudes.

ICE LAND!

Five percent of Alaska is covered by glaciers—hanging glaciers, tidewater glaciers, freshwater glaciers, valley glaciers, receding glaciers. . . . You name the glacier, Alaska probably has it!

UTAH

NEVADA

Pipe Spring National Monument

Lake Powell

Grand Canyon National Park

Colorado Plateau

Lake Mead

Mohave Museum of History and Arts

Sunset Crater Volcano National Monument

KINGMAN
Route 66 Museum

Little Colorado

Petrified Forest National Park

FLAGSTAFF

SEDONA

Verde

NEW MEXICO

LAKE HAVASU CITY

CALIFORNIA

Mogollon Rim

ARIZONA

Havasu National Wildlife Refuge

Heard Museum

Salt

PHOENIX

White Mountains

Colorado

Wildlife World Zoo

MESA

Arizona State Capitol

Gila

YUMA

Gila

Sonoran Desert

Tucson Children's Museum

San Pedro

Saguaro National Park

TUCSON

Kitt Peak National Observatory

Boothill Graveyard

NOGALES

MEXICO

N
W E
S

0   50
Miles

QUICK FACTS

State capital: Phoenix
Largest city: Phoenix
Total area: 113,998 square miles (295,255 sq km)
Highest point: Humphreys Peak, 12,633 feet (3,851 m) in Coconino County
Lowest point: 70 feet (21 m) at the Colorado River in Yuma County

ALI'S CAMEL CORPS

Syrian-born Hadji Ali helped U.S. soldiers learn to ride camels imported to build a route through the desert in the 1850s. A monument at Ali's grave in Quartzsite recognizes his service.

FROM COWS TO CASES

Sandra Day O'Connor, who became the first woman nominated to the Supreme Court in 1981, grew up on a cattle ranch in Duncan. From lassos to the law!

SUNGAZING

Kitt Peak is home to the largest solar telescope in the world. The Nicholas U. Mayall Telescope building is 187 feet tall and can be seen from 50 miles away!

LAW AND ORDER

On October 26, 1881, the famous gunfight at the O.K. Corral took place between outlaws and law officers. Wish you'd been there? Experience the showdown firsthand in Tombstone—it's reenacted daily!

OLD AS THE HILLS

Oraibi, believed to be America's oldest continuously inhabited settlement, was founded in what is now Navajo County around 1100 c.e. Go check it out but don't bother with your camera—residents don't allow photos.

SIDEWALK SNACKS

Oatman is so hot that the town hosts an egg-frying contest on its sidewalks every July 4th. But beware, contestants! Wild burros roam the town, trying to eat the entries.

GRAND GUESTS

The Grand Canyon had 44,173 visitors during its first year as a National Park in 1919. These days, it welcomes 5 million people a year from all over the world.

THE COPPER STATE

The dome of Arizona's capitol building is covered with enough copper to make 4.8 million pennies. (For you math and money fans, that's $48,000. Yowza!)

CRACK THIS!

How's this for a unique contribution? The Navajo helped America win World War II by developing a code based on their complex language that no one could crack.

BRIDGE BUY

In 1968, an Arizona businessman bought London Bridge from the British government—and had it shipped to America! The bridge was reconstructed in Lake Havasu and opened in 1971.

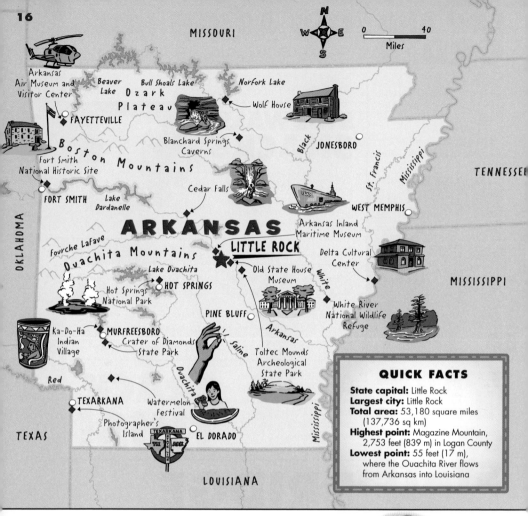

MISSOURI

N
W E
S

0   40
Miles

Arkansas Air Museum and Visitor Center

Beaver Lake

Bull Shoals Lake

Ozark Plateau

Norfork Lake

Wolf House

FAYETTEVILLE

Blanchard Springs Caverns

Black

JONESBORO

St. Francis

Mississippi

TENNESSEE

Boston Mountains

Fort Smith National Historic Site

FORT SMITH

Lake Dardanelle

Cedar Falls

USS

WEST MEMPHIS

ARKANSAS

Arkansas Inland Maritime Museum

OKLAHOMA

Fourche Lafave

Ouachita Mountains

LITTLE ROCK

Delta Cultural Center

MISSISSIPPI

Lake Ouachita

Old State House Museum

White

Hot Springs National Park

HOT SPRINGS

Ka-Do-Ha Indian Village

MURFREESBORO

Crater of Diamonds State Park

PINE BLUFF

White River National Wildlife Refuge

Arkansas

Saline

Toltec Mounds Archeological State Park

Red

Ouachita

TEXARKANA

Watermelon Festival

Photographer's Island

TEXARKANA
TX   AR

EL DORADO

Mississippi

TEXAS

LOUISIANA

QUICK FACTS

State capital: Little Rock
Largest city: Little Rock
Total area: 53,180 square miles (137,736 sq km)
Highest point: Magazine Mountain, 2,753 feet (839 m) in Logan County
Lowest point: 55 feet (17 m), where the Ouachita River flows from Arkansas into Louisiana

DIGGING FOR DIAMONDS

Feeling lucky? Try diamond hunting at the Crater of Diamonds State Park in Murfreesboro. You can keep whatever you find—no matter how big!

AMERICA'S SPA

Hot Springs National Park, known as "America's Spa," is home to... you guessed it! Hot springs! Every day, 700,000 gallons of 143° F water flows from the earth into the thermal springs.

The 1862 Battle of Pea Ridge was one of the only Civil War battles in which Native Americans participated. They fought as two Confederate regiments.

CHEROKEE CONFEDERATES

THE ARKANSAS TOOTHPICK

Before you use an Arkansas toothpick, you should know something—it's no toothpick. It's actually a dagger with a 25-inch blade. Probably best not to pick your teeth with it.

MAN IN BLACK

The legendary Johnny Cash, winner of 13 Grammy Awards and an inductee into two different halls of fame, was born in Kingsland and homegrown in Dyess.

Think your pet toad is a champion? Hop on over to Conway for the Toad Suck Daze Festival and enter your athletic amphibian in the World Championship Toad Races!

TOADALLY AWESOME!

In the winter of 1982-1983, the Griggs family of Benton hit archaeological pay dirt when they found a 300-year-old, 24-foot Indian canoe while cleaning up after the Saline River flooded their farm.

CULTURAL CANOE

HOME OF THE BRAVE

In 1957, nine African American students—known as the Little Rock Nine—attended the previously all-white Central High School in Little Rock, taking one brave, giant step for humankind.

LIGHTS, CAMERA, ACTION!

The Legend of Boggy Creek is a film about the Fouke Monster, a hairy, red-eyed "cryptid" who started haunting Arkansas residents in 1946. Real? Imaginary? You be the judge . . .

IDENTITY CRISIS

The South Arkansas Vine-Ripe Pink Tomato is the state fruit—and vegetable—of Arkansas. The tomato is considered a fruit but often used as a vegetable, so why not call it both?!

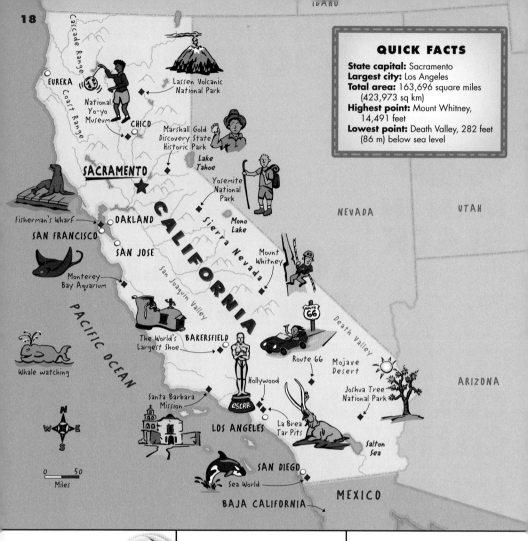

IDAHO

QUICK FACTS

State capital: Sacramento
Largest city: Los Angeles
Total area: 163,696 square miles (423,973 sq km)
Highest point: Mount Whitney, 14,491 feet
Lowest point: Death Valley, 282 feet (86 m) below sea level

Cascade Range
Coast Range
EUREKA
National Yo-yo Museum
CHICO
Lassen Volcanic National Park
Marshall Gold Discovery State Historic Park
Lake Tahoe
SACRAMENTO
Yosemite National Park
CALIFORNIA
Sierra Nevada
Mono Lake
NEVADA
UTAH
Fisherman's Wharf
OAKLAND
SAN FRANCISCO
SAN JOSE
Mount Whitney
Monterey Bay Aquarium
San Joaquin Valley
The World's Largest Shoe
BAKERSFIELD
PACIFIC OCEAN
ROUTE 66
Death Valley
Whale watching
Hollywood
Route 66
Mojave Desert
ARIZONA
Santa Barbara Mission
OSCAR
Joshua Tree National Park
LOS ANGELES
La Brea Tar Pits
Salton Sea
N W E S
SAN DIEGO
0   50
Miles
Sea World
MEXICO
BAJA CALIFORNIA

YO! YO-YOs!

In 1928, Pedro Flores started a national yo-yo craze when he made his dream of mass-producing the toy a reality and opened a factory in Santa Barbara.

TREE IN HIDING

The oldest tree in North America is believed to be in Bishop—in the Ancient Bristle Cone Pine Forest—but the exact location of the 4,600-year-old tree is kept secret, to protect it.

Do you know how many earthquakes and tremors are recorded in California each year? About half a million! Stay safe, Californians—secure those bookcases and put latches on your cabinets.

SHAKE, RATTLE, & ROLL

CABLE-ICIOUS!

The two main cables of San Francisco's Golden Gate Bridge contain 80,000 miles of steel wire. That's enough to circle the equator over three times!

FLYING RICE

Want to be a California rice farmer? Get your pilot's license. In the Golden State, rice is planted from the air, by planes flying at 100 miles per hour!

MOBILE MONUMENT

If you like to keep moving when you sightsee, head to San Francisco and check out America's only mobile national monument— the cable car. Hop on and get some history!

TALL TEMPERATURES

Baker hosts the World's Largest Thermometer. It's 134 feet tall, in honor of the hottest day in U.S. history—134 degrees in 1913, in nearby Death Valley. Sizzling!

BAKER GATEWAY TO DEATH VALLEY

CHEWY WALLS

Need somewhere to put your gum? Visit Bubble Gum Alley in San Luis Obispo, and stick it on the wall alongside more pieces of gum than anyone would ever want to count.

HIGHS AND LOWS

California has both the highest and the lowest points in the Lower 48. Weird, right? The difference between Mount Whitney (14,491 feet above sea level) and Death Valley (282 feet below sea level) is 14,773 feet!

BADWATER BASIN
282 FEET/855 METERS
BELOW SEA LEVEL

Live in California? You'd better like nuts! The Golden State produces most of the country's walnuts and almonds, thanks to places like Fresno, one of California's top agricultural counties.

GOING NUTS

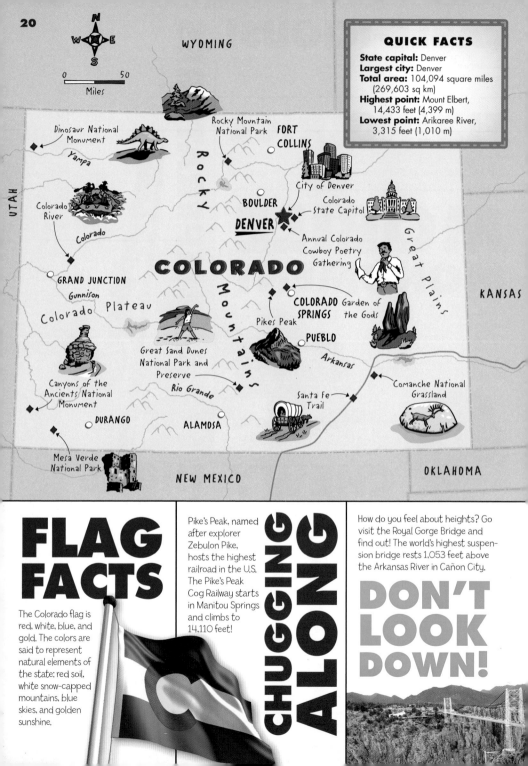

N W E S

WYOMING

0 50
Miles

QUICK FACTS

State capital: Denver
Largest city: Denver
Total area: 104,094 square miles (269,603 sq km)
Highest point: Mount Elbert, 14,433 feet (4,399 m)
Lowest point: Arikaree River, 3,315 feet (1,010 m)

Dinosaur National Monument

Rocky Mountain National Park

FORT COLLINS

City of Denver

Colorado River

Yampa

Rocky

BOULDER

DENVER

Colorado State Capitol

UTAH

Colorado

Annual Colorado Cowboy Poetry Gathering

Great Plains

COLORADO

GRAND JUNCTION

Gunnison

Plateau

Colorado

M o u n t a i n s

COLORADO SPRINGS

Pikes Peak

Garden of the Gods

KANSAS

Great Sand Dunes National Park and Preserve

PUEBLO

Rio Grande

Arkansas

Canyons of the Ancients National Monument

Santa Fe Trail

Comanche National Grassland

DURANGO

ALAMOSA

Mesa Verde National Park

NEW MEXICO

OKLAHOMA

FLAG FACTS

The Colorado flag is red, white, blue, and gold. The colors are said to represent natural elements of the state: red soil, white snow-capped mountains, blue skies, and golden sunshine.

CHUGGING ALONG

Pike's Peak, named after explorer Zebulon Pike, hosts the highest railroad in the U.S. The Pike's Peak Cog Railway starts in Manitou Springs and climbs to 14,110 feet!

How do you feel about heights? Go visit the Royal Gorge Bridge and find out! The world's highest suspension bridge rests 1,053 feet above the Arkansas River in Cañon City.

DON'T LOOK DOWN!

THE HIGH LIFE

About 1,000 years ago, ancestors of the Anasazi people built houses into the cliffs in what is now Mesa Verde National Park. There was no rolling out of bed in those houses!

ENDLESS AVENUE

The longest continuous street in America is Denver's Colfax Avenue. The 40-mile-long street has many claims to fame, including several mentions in Jack Kerouac's novel *On the Road*.

OSCAR HISTORY

Hattie McDaniel, the first African American to win an Oscar, grew up in Denver. The singer and actress appeared in over 300 films, receiving credit for only about 90.

DONKEY DASH

At the end of July in Fairplay, competitors in the Burro Days' 29-mile race must dash from downtown Fairplay to the summit of Mosquito Pass—while leading a donkey.

THE FOUR CORNERS

Can't decide where to go? Cover all your bases and head to Colorado's southwest corner where you can stand in Arizona, New Mexico, Utah, and Colorado at the same time!

UNSINKABLE, INDEED!

Activist Margaret Brown, who lived for a time in Leadville, became known posthumously as the Unsinkable Molly Brown, a reference to having survived the sinking of the *Titanic* in 1912.

CAR-PART CRITTERS

The Swetsville Zoo in Timnath was home to over 160 scrap-metal creatures including a giant car with spider legs and dinosaur-like monsters rocking out in a "heavy metal" band.

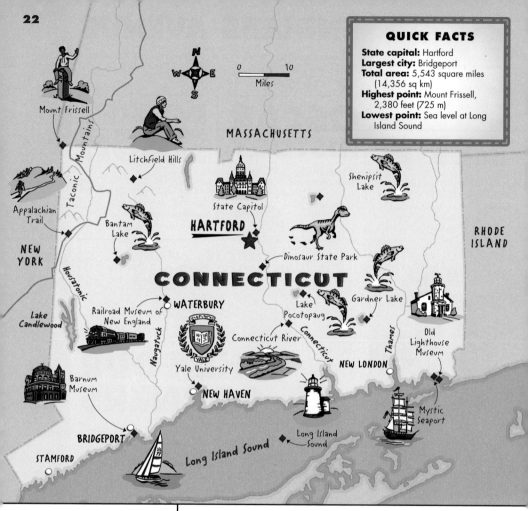

QUICK FACTS

State capital: Hartford
Largest city: Bridgeport
Total area: 5,543 square miles (14,356 sq km)
Highest point: Mount Frissell, 2,380 feet (725 m)
Lowest point: Sea level at Long Island Sound

Mount Frissell

Taconic Mountains

MASSACHUSETTS

Litchfield Hills

Appalachian Trail

NEW YORK

Bantam Lake

State Capitol

HARTFORD

Shenipsit Lake

RHODE ISLAND

CONNECTICUT

Dinosaur State Park

Housatonic

WATERBURY

Lake Pocotopaug

Gardner Lake

Railroad Museum of New England

Lake Candlewood

Naugatuck

Yale University

Connecticut River

Connecticut

Thames

NEW LONDON

Old Lighthouse Museum

Barnum Museum

NEW HAVEN

Mystic Seaport

BRIDGEPORT

Long Island Sound

Long Island Sound

STAMFORD

WHAT'S IN A NAME?

If you were trying to name a town that was halfway between Hartford and New Haven, what would you name it? Hmm, that's a tough one. How about... Middletown?!

GENIUS INVENTION!

A father and semi-pro pitcher from Fairfield invented Wiffle Ball for his son, whose arm hurt from trying to prevent broken windows by throwing a golf ball instead of a baseball.

T.KEELER's INN

SEEING IS BELIEVING

Looking for tangible evidence of the Revolutionary War? Go to the Keeler Tavern Museum in Ridgefield, where a British cannonball is still lodged in one of the tavern's beams!

BIG! HUGE! JUMBO?

Circus showman P.T. Barnum of Bethel introduced the word "jumbo" into American English when he imported a supersized elephant named Jumbo from London in 1882.

DINOSAUR DISCOVERY

Rocky Hill is home to 2,000 dinosaur footprints. Workers excavating a site for a new building found the 200-million-year-old tracks by accident! Now the site is a Registered Natural Landmark.

In 1687, as British officials argued with Connecticut lawmakers over the colony's charter, Captain Joseph Wadsworth grabbed the document and hid it in an oak tree for safekeeping.

THE CHARTER OAK

SAY WHAT?

In 1806, Thomas Jefferson sued *The Hartford Courant* for libel when the paper wrote that Jefferson bribed French officials to win their support. Jefferson lost the case in the Supreme Court.

B-BALL FOR ALL

The University of Connecticut is the first state university to have both its men's and women's basketball teams win NCAA championships in the same year. Go, Huskies!

BILLIONS OF PEZ

Americans love their PEZ—they eat 3 billion of the sweet treats a year! Manufactured in Orange, PEZ is as famous for its dispensers as for its sugary taste.

WORDSMITH WEBSTER

Next time you look up a word, think of smarty-pants Noah Webster from Hartford, author of the first American dictionary, published in 1828. (How did he know all those words?!)

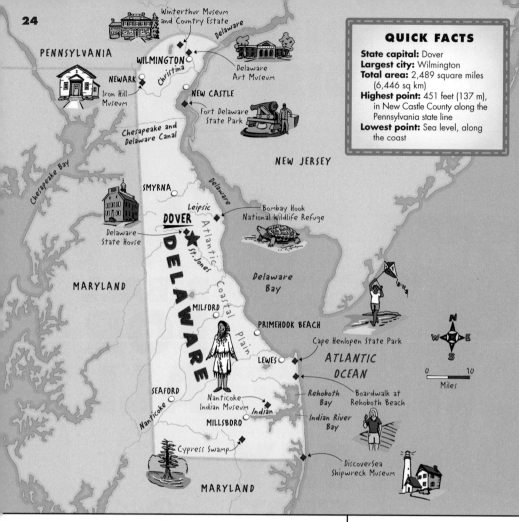

PENNSYLVANIA

Winterthur Museum and Country Estate

WILMINGTON

Delaware

NEWARK

Iron Hill Museum

Christina

Delaware Art Museum

NEW CASTLE

Fort Delaware State Park

Chesapeake and Delaware Canal

Chesapeake Bay

NEW JERSEY

SMYRNA

Delaware

DOVER

Leipsic

Bombay Hook National Wildlife Refuge

Delaware State House

DELAWARE

St. Jones

Atlantic

Coastal Plain

MARYLAND

Delaware Bay

MILFORD

PRIMEHOOK BEACH

Cape Henlopen State Park

LEWES

ATLANTIC OCEAN

N
W E
S

0   10
Miles

SEAFORD

Nanticoke Indian Museum

Indian

MILLSBORO

Rehoboth Bay

Boardwalk at Rehoboth Beach

Indian River Bay

Nanticoke

Cypress Swamp

DiscoverSea Shipwreck Museum

MARYLAND

QUICK FACTS

State capital: Dover
Largest city: Wilmington
Total area: 2,489 square miles (6,446 sq km)
Highest point: 451 feet (137 m), in New Castle County along the Pennsylvania state line
Lowest point: Sea level, along the coast

WATER POWER

The famous American chemical company DuPont had modest beginnings in 1802 as a gunpowder factory powered by the steep drop in elevation of the Brandywine River.

#1 STATE

Delaware, the "First State," was the first of the original thirteen colonies to ratify the U.S. Constitution. Ratification took place in 1787 at Dover's Golden Fleece Tavern.

A GOOD CITIZEN

Thomas Garrett, a Quaker iron merchant from Wilmington, lost everything when a court fined him for helping 2,000 slaves to freedom on the Underground Railroad. He continued his work anyway.

MONSTER MONUMENT

The 46-foot-tall Miles the Monster at the Dover International Speedway is one of the tallest fiberglass structures anywhere. He even has a full-sized stock car in one hand!

FIT FOR A QUEEN

The Christina River, named after a queen of Sweden, has had more than 25 names over the years, including Christeen Creek, Christiany River, Minquaas Kill, and Sickpeckons.

SQUISHED SQUASH!

Every year around Halloween, people gather in Bridgeville and use catapults and other machines to fling pumpkins far and wide—the record is 3,000 feet!—in the World Championship Punkin' Chunkin'.

LET'S SPLIT IT!

Delmar is known as "the little town too big for one state"—it's in both Delaware and Maryland (hence the name). The state line runs right down the center of town!

FOR REAL?

Delaware has exactly zero acres of land run by the National Park Service. (The national parks along the Delaware River are in New Jersey, New York, and Pennsylvania.)

BATTLE FOR THE BRIDGE

The Battle of Cooch's Bridge was the only Revolutionary War battle fought in Delaware. Legend has it that the 13-star flag was flown for the first time in this battle.

BIG DEAL

Why would someone who lives in New Jersey, Maryland, or Pennsylvania drive all the way to Delaware just to shop? Because there's no sales tax!

ALABAMA

Florida Panhandle

GEORGIA

State Capitol

ATLANTIC OCEAN

PENSACOLA

★ TALLAHASSEE

St. Augustine

JACKSONVILLE

Gulf Islands National Seashore

F L O R I D A

Daytona International Speedway

OCALA

UNIVERSAL

Universal Orlando

John F. Kennedy Space Center

N W E S

Plant City

Florida Peninsula

ORLANDO

GULF OF MEXICO

TAMPA

PLANT CITY

Walt Disney World/ EPCOT/ MGM Studios

0   50
Miles

ST. PETERSBURG

Bok Tower

The John and Mable Ringling Museum of Art

SARASOTA

WEST PALM BEACH

The Villa Vizcaya Museum and Gardens

QUICK FACTS

State capital: Tallahassee
Largest city: Jacksonville
Total area: 65,755 square miles
(170,305 sq km)
Highest point: In Walton County,
345 feet (105 m) above sea level
Lowest point: Sea level along the
Atlantic Ocean

Sanibel Island

MIAMI

Everglades National Park

Miami Beach

KEY WEST

Florida Keys

SOFT AND STRONG

The walls of the 17th century fort Castillo de San Marcos, in St. Augustine, were made of coquina, a type of soft limestone that could actually absorb cannonballs!

CATFISH CROSSING

Look both ways when you're crossing the road in Florida. You might catch sight of the Asian catfish *Clarias batrachus* making its way across the street. (No, we're not kidding.)

Clearwater has the highest rate of lightning strikes per capita. Clearwater residents who work outdoors in spring, summer, or fall are more likely to be struck than Americans anywhere else!

LOOK OUT!

CUSTOM MADE WEATHER

The Vehicle Assembly Building at Cape Canaveral's Kennedy Space Center has such a high ceiling that rain clouds form inside on humid days!

HAPPY NEW YEAR!

If you were in Tampa on January 1, 1914, your New Year's resolution could have been to take the first flight on the country's first commercial airline, the St. Petersburg-Tampa Airboat Line.

TANNING HISTORY

Miami Beach pharmacist Benjamin Green invented suntan lotion in 1944 by cooking cocoa butter on a stove and testing it on his head. He called it Coppertone Suntan Cream.

STORY TIME

Some of the highest paid workers in Ybor City's cigar factories never touched a cigar. They read aloud to the workers, who contributed weekly to pay the reader.

DR. ICE

It makes sense that the man who popularized ice came from one of the hottest states in the country! Dr. John Gorrie of Apalachicola patented an ice machine in 1851.

GATOR AID!

In 1965, a professor at the University of Florida in Gainesville invented Gatorade when the school's football players suffered from dehydration. Where did the name come from? Gator, the school's mascot!

The Everglades is the only place on earth where alligators and crocodiles live side by side. Does that make you want to visit—or stay far away? Hard to say . . .

CRAZY COHABITATION

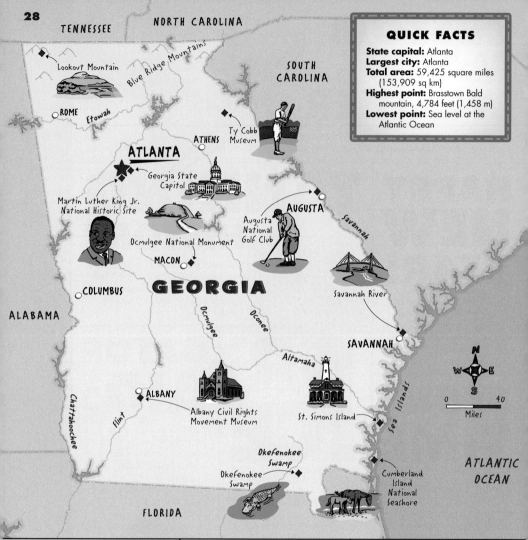

TENNESSEE
NORTH CAROLINA
SOUTH CAROLINA
Lookout Mountain
Blue Ridge Mountains
ROME
Etowah
ATHENS
Ty Cobb Museum
ATLANTA
Georgia State Capitol
Martin Luther King Jr. National Historic Site
Ocmulgee National Monument
AUGUSTA
Augusta National Golf Club
Savannah
MACON
COLUMBUS
GEORGIA
Ocmulgee
Oconee
Savannah River
ALABAMA
SAVANNAH
Altamaha
ALBANY
Albany Civil Rights Movement Museum
St. Simons Island
Chattahoochee
Flint
Sea Islands
Okefenokee Swamp
Okefenokee Swamp
Cumberland Island National Seashore
FLORIDA
ATLANTIC OCEAN

N W E S

0   40
Miles

QUICK FACTS

State capital: Atlanta
Largest city: Atlanta
Total area: 59,425 square miles (153,909 sq km)
Highest point: Brasstown Bald mountain, 4,784 feet (1,458 m)
Lowest point: Sea level at the Atlantic Ocean

GOLD GREED

Cherokee Indian culture flourished in Georgia until the Georgia Gold Rush started in Dahlonega in 1829. By 1838, the Native Americans had been forced to leave their land.

HISTORIC HOSPITAL BIRTH

Peanut farmer Jimmy Carter was the first U.S. president to be born in a hospital! He was born in Plains.

SWEET Ps

Georgia is full of yummy things to snack on, and most of them start with the letter "p"! The state is among the country's top producers of peanuts, peaches, and pecans.

BIZARRE BABIES

Babyland General Hospital in Cleveland is the birthplace of all Cabbage Patch Kids. It has a maternity ward, a nursery, and a gift shop where visitors can "adopt" a doll.

Blackbeard Island is named after Edward "Blackbeard" Teach, a legendary pirate who is rumored to have buried his treasure on the island. His loot remains to be found, treasure hunters!

BURIED TREASURE

GRANITE GENERALS

Stone Mountain is the world's largest mass of exposed granite, making it the ideal place for the world's largest high-relief sculpture! The Confederate Memorial Carving is bigger than a football field.

NAME AND RENAME

Atlanta was originally called Terminus in 1837, because the area was quickly developing around a new railroad that was going to "terminate," or end, there. (Frankly, we like "Atlanta" better.)

REUNION THROUGH SONG

An American anthropologist connected Mary Moran of Harris Neck with long-lost relatives in Sierra Leone through a song brought over by enslaved Africans and passed down through generations.

Okefenokee Swamp is about 7,000 years old, and home to over 400 species of animals! Okefenokee is a Choctaw Indian word meaning "land of the trembling earth."

WILD (LIFE) REFUGE

SODA'S STORY

In 1886, pharmacist and chemist John Stith Pemberton invented Coca-Cola in Atlanta. It was originally called Pemberton's French Wine Coca—because it had wine in it!

GEORGIA

THE PEACH STATE

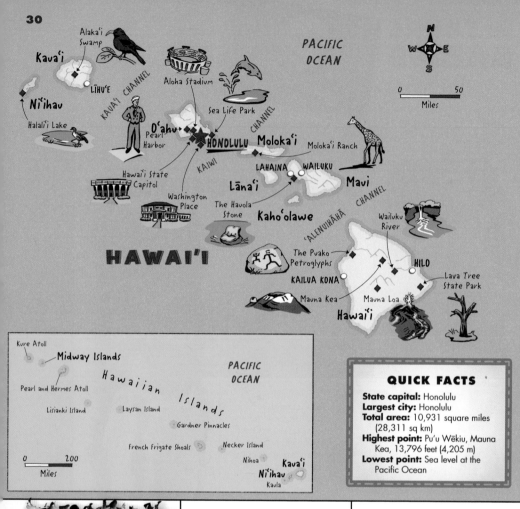

Kaua'i
Alaka'i Swamp
LĪHU'E
KAUA'I CHANNEL
Aloha Stadium
PACIFIC OCEAN
N W E S

0 50 Miles

Ni'ihau
Halali'i Lake
O'ahu
Pearl Harbor
Sea Life Park
KAIWI
HONOLULU
Moloka'i
Moloka'i Ranch
Hawai'i State Capitol
Washington Place
LAHAINA
WAILUKU
Lāna'i
The Hauola Stone
Kaho'olawe
Maui
'ALENUIHĀHĀ CHANNEL
Wailuku River

HAWAI'I

The Puako Petroglyphs
KAILUA KONA
Mauna Kea
Mauna Loa
HILO
Lava Tree State Park
Hawai'i

Kure Atoll
Midway Islands
Pearl and Hermes Atoll
Hawaiian Islands
PACIFIC OCEAN
Lisianki Island
Laysan Island
Gardner Pinnacles
French Frigate Shoals
Necker Island
Nihoa
Kaua'i
Ni'ihau
Kaula

0 200 Miles

QUICK FACTS

State capital: Honolulu
Largest city: Honolulu
Total area: 10,931 square miles (28,311 sq km)
Highest point: Pu'u Wēkiu, Mauna Kea, 13,796 feet (4,205 m)
Lowest point: Sea level at the Pacific Ocean

FLOWERS FOR FRIENDS

On May 1, Hawaiian friends give each other leis for Lei Day. The tradition started in the late 1920s, and even has its own song—"May Day is Lei Day in Hawai'i."

SUMO STAR

In 1972, Jesse James Wailani Kuhaulua, a former high school football player, became the first non-Japanese athlete to be a sumo champion. He competed for 20 years—unheard of in wrestling!

WHOLPHIN WONDER!

The first wholphin was born in captivity at Sea Life Park in 1985 to a bottlenose dolphin and a whale. Take the backstage tour at the park to meet her!

NO JOKE

On April Fools Day in 1946, children from Laupahoehoe reported that the ocean disappeared. People thought they were kidding, but they weren't—they were witnessing a tsunami.

LONG-TERM LAVA

Hawaiʻi's volcano Kilauea is the most active volcano in the world. It started erupting on January 3, 1983, and it hasn't stopped since. That's a lot of lava!

MACADAMIA MADNESS

Sugar plantation manager William H. Purvis brought macadamia tree seeds to Hawaiʻi from Australia in 1881 and unknowingly gave Hawaiʻi one of its most famous products!

AMERICA'S PALACE

The only palace on American soil is the ʻIolani Royal Palace in Honolulu, built in 1882. It was home to the last two rulers of the Kingdom of Hawaiʻi.

COFFEE-LOVERS PARADISE

Hawaiʻi is the only place in the United States that grows coffee, producing 6 to 7 million pounds of coffee beans per year.

EXTRAORDINARY ELVIS!

Rock star and soldier Elvis Presley donated over $50,000 in proceeds from his 1961 Honolulu concert to help build the USS *Arizona* War Memorial, commemorating those who died at Pearl Harbor.

DUKE OF FIRSTS

Duke Paoa Kahinu Mokoe Hulikohola Kahanamoku won an Olympic gold medal for Hawaiʻi in 1912 in the 100-meter freestyle. He was also America's first surfing star. Hang ten, Duke!

CANADA

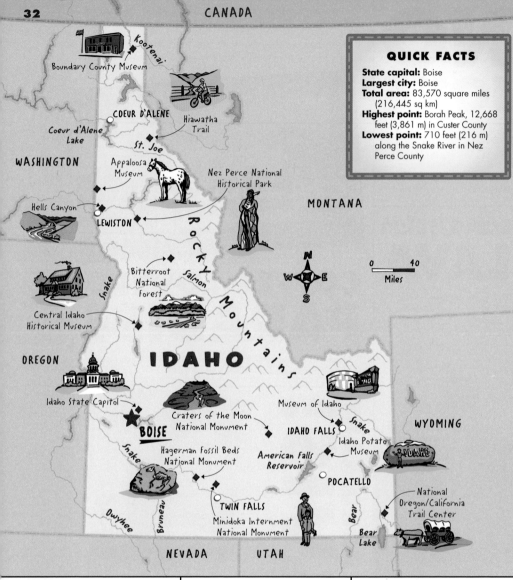

Boundary County Museum

COEUR D'ALENE

Hiawatha Trail

Coeur d'Alene Lake

Kootenai

St. Joe

WASHINGTON

Appaloosa Museum

Nez Perce National Historical Park

MONTANA

Hells Canyon

LEWISTON

Snake

Central Idaho Historical Museum

Bitterroot National Forest

Salmon

Rocky Mountains

OREGON

IDAHO

Idaho State Capitol

Craters of the Moon National Monument

Museum of Idaho

WYOMING

BOISE

Hagerman Fossil Beds National Monument

American Falls Reservoir

IDAHO FALLS

Snake

Idaho Potato Museum

IDAHO

Snake

POCATELLO

National Oregon/California Trail Center

Owyhee

Bruneau

TWIN FALLS

Minidoka Internment National Monument

Bear

Bear Lake

NEVADA

UTAH

QUICK FACTS

State capital: Boise
Largest city: Boise
Total area: 83,570 square miles (216,445 sq km)
Highest point: Borah Peak, 12,668 feet (3,861 m) in Custer County
Lowest point: 710 feet (216 m) along the Snake River in Nez Perce County

N W E S

0   40
Miles

IN HOT WATER

The Idaho Capitol Building is heated by hot water pumped up from 3,000 feet underground. It's the only capitol building in the nation that's warmed by a geothermal well!

HOME OF HOKEY

Legend has it that songwriter Larry LaPrise and pals wrote "The Hokey Pokey" in 1949 to entertain Sun Valley skiers. "Put your left ski in, put your left ski out . . ."

CANYON STATS

Hell's Canyon, North America's deepest river gorge, is 10 miles wide and more than 8,000 feet below He Devil Peak, the top of Idaho's Seven Devils Mountains. That's deep, all right.

HORSE HISTORY

The Hagerman Fossil Beds is home to the Hagerman Horse Quarry, the largest concentration of horse fossils in North America. Some consider it the most important horse history site in the world.

MOON ON EARTH

In 1969, the Apollo 14 crew went to the moon without leaving the earth! How? They visited Craters of the Moon National Monument to prepare for their trip into space.

RIVERS GALORE

Idaho has 3,100 miles of rivers, which is more than any other state. So if you live in Idaho but you don't like the water, consider moving just about anywhere else!

GIANT CRUNCH

Are you a potato chip fanatic? Go visit the world's largest potato chip in the Idaho Potato Museum in Blackfoot. It's 14 inches by 25 inches; that should satisfy your cravings!

IDAHO POTATO MUSEUM
BLACKFOOT IDAHO

BALANCING ACT

Balanced Rock, near Buhl, is 48-feet high, weighs 40 tons, and rests on a base that is 3 feet by 17 inches. Think twice before you sit under it!

Philo T. Farnsworth first sketched his invention—the television—for a teacher on a chalkboard at Rigby High School when he was 14 years old. How's that for precocious?

DYNAMIC DOODLE

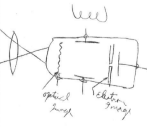

LUCKY LEAPER

In 1974, motorcycle daredevil Evel Knievel tried to jump Snake River Canyon. The results were disastrous and Knievel crashed. However, in daredevil fashion, he walked away with only minor injuries.

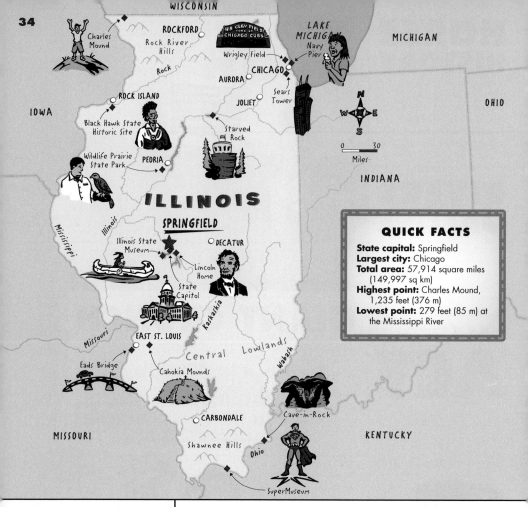

WISCONSIN

Charles Mound

ROCKFORD
Rock River Hills

Rock

WRIGLEY FIELD
HOME OF THE
CHICAGO CUBS
Wrigley field

LAKE MICHIGAN
Navy Pier

MICHIGAN

AURORA
CHICAGO

Sears Tower

JOLIET

IOWA

ROCK ISLAND

Black Hawk State Historic Site

Starved Rock

OHIO

Wildlife Prairie State Park
PEORIA

ILLINOIS

SPRINGFIELD

Illinois State Museum

DECATUR

Lincoln Home

State Capitol

Kaskaskia

INDIANA

Mississippi

Illinois

0   30
Miles

Missouri

EAST ST. LOUIS

Central Lowlands

Wabash

Eads Bridge

Cahokia Mounds

CARBONDALE

Cave-in-Rock

KENTUCKY

MISSOURI

Shawnee Hills

Ohio

SuperMuseum

QUICK FACTS

State capital: Springfield
Largest city: Chicago
Total area: 57,914 square miles (149,997 sq km)
Highest point: Charles Mound, 1,235 feet (376 m)
Lowest point: 279 feet (85 m) at the Mississippi River

WONDERFUL WHEEL

The Ferris Wheel debuted at the 1893 Chicago World's Fair, designed by George Ferris of Galesburg. It was 250 feet tall and had 36 wooden cars, which each held 60 passengers!

WACKY WATER

Every year, the Chicago River magically turns emerald green on St. Patrick's Day! (Well, not quite magically—a man named Mike Butler dyes the river in honor of the holiday.)

INNOCENT COW!

In 1871, a newspaper blamed Mrs. O'Leary's cow for kicking over the lantern that started the Great Chicago Fire, but a reporter later confessed to making up the story.

SPECTACULAR SUE!

Visit the world's largest Tyrannosaurus Rex skeleton in the Field Museum in Chicago. Her name is Sue—after the fossil hunter who found her—and she's 67 million years old!

LOOPY LAB

In 1942, Enrico Fermi built the first nuclear reactor, working in a lab that had previously been a squash court under Stagg Field, the University of Chicago's football stadium.

CATSUP CAPER

The World's Largest Catsup Bottle stands 170 feet tall in Collinsville. But don't bother visiting the bottle with your burger—it's just a water tower. Bummer!

FABULOUS FASTENER

The hookless fastener that keeps our pants up on a daily basis—aka the zipper—was invented in Chicago in 1891. Can you imagine a world without zippers? We can't, either.

Illinois has one of the highest numbers of personalized—or vanity—license plates in the nation. That's a lot of "vanitized" cars!

ILLINOIS IS GR8!

MAKING IT UP

Before he was president, Tampico-born broadcaster Ronald Reagan improvised the events of a 1934 Chicago Cubs game for listeners when the wire that was feeding him information went dead!

SUPER OBSESSION

A 15-foot-tall, two-ton sculpture of Superman watches over Metropolis—naturally! The town proclaims itself the "Hometown of Superman" and even has a newspaper called *The Planet!*

LAKE MICHIGAN

MICHIGAN

LAKE ERIE

National New York Central Railroad Museum

SOUTH BEND

GARY

Indiana Dunes National Lakeshore

National College Football Hall of Fame

Hoosier Buggy Shop

Kankakee

FORT WAYNE

Maumee

Foellinger-Freimann Botanical Conservatory

Jasper-Pulaski State fish and Wildlife Area

Quilters Hall of Fame

Wabash

LAFAYETTE

MUNCIE

ILLINOIS

INDIANA

N
W   E
S

0   30
Miles

Ernie Pyle State Historic Site

INDIANAPOLIS

Indiana State Capitol

OHIO

TERRE HAUTE

Indiana University

BLOOMINGTON

Eiteljorg Museum of American Indians and Western Art

West Fork White

East Fork White

Ohio

George Rogers Clark National Historical Park

Marengo Cave National Landmark

Wabash

Lincoln Boyhood National Memorial

NEW ALBANY

EVANSVILLE

KENTUCKY

Ohio

Wyandotte Caves State Recreation Area

QUICK FACTS

State capital: Indianapolis
Largest city: Indianapolis
Total area: 36,418 square miles (94,322 sq km)
Highest point: Hoosier Hill, 1,257 feet (383 m), in Wayne County
Lowest point: Along the Ohio River, 320 feet (98 m)

NO PHOTOS, PLEASE!

According to published accounts, when the Secret Service stopped *Indianapolis News* photographer Paul Shideler from taking President Herbert Hoover's photo, the paper complained, and the press won the right to photograph the president.

Martinsville was home to America's first successful goldfish farm, the Grassyfork Fisheries. Within 50 years of opening in 1899, it produced 25 million fish a year!

FISH GOLD!

TORNADO TORMENT

Tornadoes have struck Indiana in every month of the year. So much for tornado season! The state sees an average of about 23 tornadoes annually.

MAKEUP MILLIONAIRE!

Indianapolis entrepreneur and social activist Madam C.J. Walker became one of America's first female millionaires in the early 1900s by manufacturing cosmetics for black women. She started her business by going door-to-door.

TASTY TREATS

In one year, Indiana produced more than 192.5 million pounds of popcorn and 68 million gallons of ice cream. Now THAT'S a great claim to fame!

ALL ABOARD

The Fountain City home of Quaker abolitionists Levi and Catharine Coffin was a very busy stop on the Underground Railroad—so busy, in fact, that it was nicknamed Grand Central Station.

SPECIAL STONE

Several of the country's most famous buildings were constructed with Indiana limestone, including the Pentagon, the Empire State Building—and the new Yankee Stadium!

TRAIN THIEVES

The notorious Reno Gang committed the first U.S. train robbery when they jumped a train leaving Seymour and stole $12,000. (That's about $164,000 in today's economy.)

LET THERE BE...

Wabash became the first American city to have electric streetlamps in 1880. The cost for one year was $712, and the city council was thrilled with such "marvelous cheapness."

SECOND TO ONE

WELCOME TO HUNTINGTON HOME OF THE 44TH VICE PRESIDENT DAN QUAYLE

Indiana is known as the "Mother of Vice-Presidents," having produced five, including Dan Quayle, whose museum in Huntington boasts the slogan "Second to One."

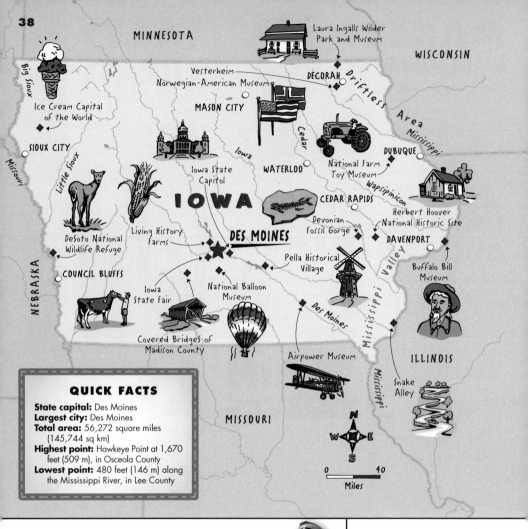

MINNESOTA

WISCONSIN

Laura Ingalls Wilder Park and Museum

Driftless Area

Big Sioux

Ice Cream Capital of the World

Vesterheim Norwegian-American Museum

DECORAH

Cedar

MASON CITY

SIOUX CITY

Little Sioux

Iowa State Capitol

Iowa

WATERLOO

DUBUQUE

Mississippi

National Farm Toy Museum

Wapsipinicon

Missouri

IOWA

CEDAR RAPIDS

Herbert Hoover National Historic Site

DeSoto National Wildlife Refuge

Living History Farms

DES MOINES

Devonian Fossil Gorge

DAVENPORT

Buffalo Bill Museum

COUNCIL BLUFFS

Pella Historical Village

Iowa State Fair

National Balloon Museum

Des Moines

NEBRASKA

Mississippi Valley

ILLINOIS

Covered Bridges of Madison County

Airpower Museum

Snake Alley

Mississippi

MISSOURI

QUICK FACTS

State capital: Des Moines
Largest city: Des Moines
Total area: 56,272 square miles (145,744 sq km)
Highest point: Hawkeye Point at 1,670 feet (509 m), in Osceola County
Lowest point: 480 feet (146 m) along the Mississippi River, in Lee County

N
W
E
S

0   40
Miles

4-H FOUNDER

Jessie Field Shambaugh of Shenandoah started the boys and girls clubs that ultimately became the 4-H Club. She also developed the four-leaf clover design that now represents the club nationally.

Every year, the citizens of LeClaire have a tug-of-war over the Mississippi River with their neighbors in Port Byron, IL. The event requires a 2,400-foot, 680-pound rope!

HUGE HOAX

In 1862, a fossilized 10-foot-tall man was discovered in New York. People flipped out—until it was revealed that "the giant" had been carved out of gypsum from Fort Dodge.

TUG FEST

BEST BEARD

Hans Langseth, from Norway, is buried in Kensett—well, most of him is. His 17-foot, 6-inch beard, which is considered the longest in the world, is proudly displayed in the Smithsonian.

OBELISK OF HONOR

Sioux City's 100-foot-tall obelisk commemorates Sergeant Charles Floyd, the only fatality of the nearly two-and-a-half-year-long Lewis and Clark expedition.

BUTTERY BOVINE

Butter Cow, the annual giant cow sculpture at the Iowa State Fair, is made with about 600 pounds of butter. She can provide butter for approximately 19,200 slices of toast!

BIG BERRY

The world's largest strawberry can be found in Strawberry Point, outside City Hall. It's 15 feet tall! (It's also made of fiberglass, so don't try to eat it.)

HEARTLAND ART

The 1930 painting *American Gothic* by Grant Wood of Cedar Rapids features a farmer and his daughter (and a pitchfork). The models for his painting? His sister and his dentist.

MODEST BEGINNINGS

When the Ringling brothers saw a circus being unloaded at the docks in McGregor, they decided to start their own circus—in their backyard. And the rest is history!

TRAGIC TRUMPETER

Davenport's mysterious Bix Beiderbecke was one of the best trumpet players who ever lived. The self-taught jazz musician and composer—"golden boy" to his friends—died at age 28.

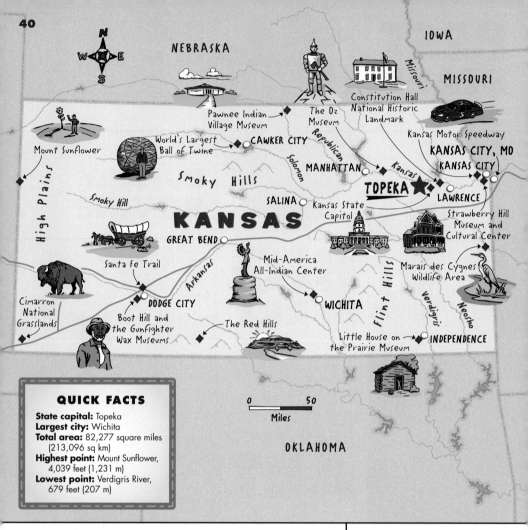

NEBRASKA

IOWA

MISSOURI

Pawnee Indian Village Museum

The Oz Museum

Constitution Hall National Historic Landmark

Kansas Motor Speedway

World's Largest Ball of Twine

CAWKER CITY

Mount Sunflower

KANSAS CITY, MO

KANSAS CITY

Republican

Missouri

Smoky Hills

MANHATTAN

Solomon

Kansas

TOPEKA

LAWRENCE

High Plains

Smoky Hill

SALINA

Kansas State Capitol

Strawberry Hill Museum and Cultural Center

KANSAS

GREAT BEND

Santa Fe Trail

Marais des Cygnes Wildlife Area

Arkansas

Mid-America All-Indian Center

Flint Hills

Verdigris

Neosho

Cimarron National Grasslands

DODGE CITY

Boot Hill and the Gunfighter Wax Museums

The Red Hills

WICHITA

Little House on the Prairie Museum

INDEPENDENCE

OKLAHOMA

0   50
Miles

QUICK FACTS

State capital: Topeka
Largest city: Wichita
Total area: 82,277 square miles (213,096 sq km)
Highest point: Mount Sunflower, 4,039 feet (1,231 m)
Lowest point: Verdigris River, 679 feet (207 m)

CENTRAL U.S.A.

Smith County is smack in the middle of the country—literally! (Okay, okay, only if you don't count Hawai'i and Alaska.)

POWERFUL "BOOKS"

Beecher's Bibles aren't bibles—they're guns! The nickname was given to rifles used by antislavery factions in pre-Civil War Kansas to honor abolitionist Henry Ward Beecher.

WINDIEST CITY

Dodge City, a town so dangerous in the late 1800s that it was famous for its cemetery, now distinguishes itself by being America's windiest city, with average winds of 13.9 mph.

KANSAS

WELL MADE WELL

Greensburg is home to the largest hand-excavated well in the world. It's 109 feet deep and 32 feet wide, and in 2008 it became one of the 8 Wonders of Kansas.

8 wonders of Kansas!

KANSAS SAMPLER FOUNDATION ©

SHOESTRING BUDGET

Frugal farmer Frank Stoeber left his fellow Cawker City citizens quite a legacy when he died: the world's largest ball of sisal twine. It's currently 40 feet around, and weighs 14,587 pounds!

ON HER OWN TERMS

In 1978, Senator Nancy Kassebaum of Topeka became the first woman elected to the U.S. Senate who was not succeeding her husband. You go, girl—or rather, well done, Senator!

DRY WIT

The 19th-century explorer Zebulon Pike had his own name for the area we now call Kansas: The Great American Desert. (Okay, so it's a little dry in Kansas. So what?!)

MARIACHI (GRAND) MAMA

In 1977, Teresa Cuevas of Topeka founded Mariachi Estrella, one of the first all-female mariachi bands. As of 2008, the 88-year-old violinist was still playing with her band.

A GOOD INVESTMENT

In 1958, two brothers borrowed $600 from their mom to open Pizza Hut in Wichita. It became an international chain, earning millions annually. Think their mom got her money back?

OLDER THAN DIRT

Hutchinson hosts what may be the world's longest living organism. An ancient salt crystal at the Kansas Underground Salt Museum contains bacteria with cells that were alive before the dinosaurs!

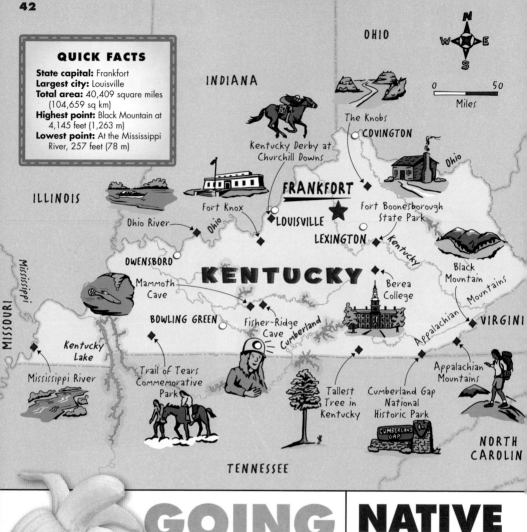

QUICK FACTS

State capital: Frankfort
Largest city: Louisville
Total area: 40,409 square miles (104,659 sq km)
Highest point: Black Mountain at 4,145 feet (1,263 m)
Lowest point: At the Mississippi River, 257 feet (78 m)

OHIO

INDIANA

The Knobs

COVINGTON

Ohio

Kentucky Derby at Churchill Downs

0   50
Miles

ILLINOIS

FRANKFORT

Fort Knox

Ohio River

Ohio

LOUISVILLE

Fort Boonesborough State Park

LEXINGTON

Kentucky

Missouri

OWENSBORO

KENTUCKY

Black Mountain

Mammoth Cave

Berea College

Mountains

MISSOURI

BOWLING GREEN

Fisher-Ridge Cave

Cumberland

Appalachian

VIRGINIA

Kentucky Lake

Mississippi River

Trail of Tears Commemorative Park

Tallest Tree in Kentucky

Cumberland Gap National Historic Park

Appalachian Mountains

CUMBERLAND GAP

NORTH CAROLINA

TENNESSEE

GOING BANANAS

The 1981 International Banana Festival in Fulton featured a one-ton banana pudding! Was that before or after they added the whipped cream?

NATIVE SONS AT ODDS

President Abraham Lincoln was born near Hodgenville, just about 100 miles from Fairview, where Confederate President Jefferson Davis was born. Statues of both stand in the Kentucky capitol building.

HISTORY THIEVES

In 2004, four men used a Taser to steal rare manuscripts from Transylvania University. The theft is considered the first armed robbery of historic documents in the U.S.

CHAMPION HORSE

Considered by many to be the greatest racehorse of all time, Man o' War was born in Lexington. He won 20 out of 21 races, though he never competed in the Kentucky Derby.

TONS OF GOLD

The Fort Knox Kentucky Bullion Depository is part of the Treasury Department. Its fortified vault holds about 4,603 tons of gold bullion. But don't bother dropping by; the facility is closed to visitors!

HOCKEY HIGHTAILS IT

Stephen Foster, the "father of American music," wrote "My Old Kentucky Home," the state's official song. What's weird about this? He never even lived in Kentucky!

JUST MAKE IT UP

SIBLING STARS

Kentucky natives and sisters Loretta Lynn and Crystal Gayle both found fame as singers. Loretta, 17 years older than Crystal, often brought her little sister on tour with her.

The Lexington-based Kentucky Thoroughblades were part of the American Hockey League from 1996–2001. When Kentuckians lost interest in the cold-weather sport, the Thoroughblades split town for Cleveland, Ohio.

HILLERICH HOMERUN

Bud Hillerich changed baseball forever after seeing pro Pete Browning break his bat during a game. Bud made Pete a new bat in his father's woodshop, and the Louisville Slugger was born!

MELTING-POT MINING

In 1917, the U.S. Coal & Coke Company built the world's largest coal-mining operation, Portal 31. It had 10,000 employees from 38 nations, and provided health care and education.

KENTUCKY

THE BLUEGRASS STATE

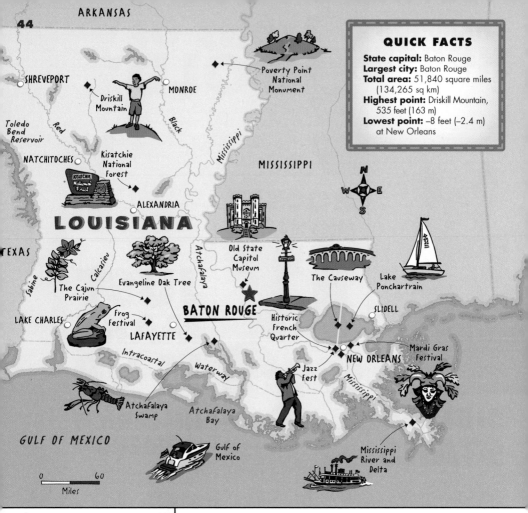

QUICK FACTS

State capital: Baton Rouge
Largest city: Baton Rouge
Total area: 51,840 square miles
(134,265 sq km)
Highest point: Driskill Mountain,
535 feet (163 m)
Lowest point: –8 feet (–2.4 m)
at New Orleans

ARKANSAS

SHREVEPORT
Driskill Mountain
MONROE
Poverty Point National Monument
Toledo Bend Reservoir
Red
Black
Mississippi
NATCHITOCHES
Kisatchie National Forest
ALEXANDRIA
LOUISIANA
MISSISSIPPI
TEXAS
Sabine
Calcasieu
The Cajun Prairie
Evangeline Oak Tree
Atchafalaya
Old State Capitol Museum
The Causeway
Lake Ponchartrain
LAKE CHARLES
Frog Festival
BATON ROUGE
Historic French Quarter
SLIDELL
LAFAYETTE
Intracoastal
Waterway
Jazz Fest
NEW ORLEANS
Mardi Gras Festival
Atchafalaya Swamp
Atchafalaya Bay
Mississippi
GULF OF MEXICO
Gulf of Mexico
Mississippi River and Delta

0 — 60
Miles

RED, HOT, & SPICY!

Edmund McIlhenny invented Tabasco sauce in 1868—he decided people needed some pep in their food as they struggled through Reconstruction. His family still produces it today!

NEVER-ENDING KNOCKOUT

The longest boxing match on record lasted more than seven hours in New Orleans in 1893. The boxers were so tired, the match had to be declared a draw.

EPIC BRIDGE

Metairie is home to the world's longest bridge over water. The Lake Pontchartrain Causeway is 24 miles long and it reportedly takes an average of 26 minutes to drive over it!

CAPITAL CAPITOL

At 450 feet, the Louisiana State Capitol in Baton Rouge is the tallest of the capitols in the United States. The art deco building is adorned with sculptures depicting the state's history.

PRESIDENTIAL PARDON

In 1815, Frenchman Jean Lafitte helped defeat the British at the Battle of New Orleans and later received a presidential pardon. Why did he need a pardon? He was a pirate!

CH-CH-CHING!

Louisiana produces 90% of the nation's crawfish, which has been in the area for centuries. Between commercial fishing and crawfish farming, the freshwater crustacean brings the state $120 million a year!

GET IT STRAIGHT!

Natchitoches, the oldest city in the Louisiana Purchase Territory, was founded in 1714. Don't confuse it with Nacogdoches, Texas, which is about 100 miles away—locals will get very upset!

LOTSA LAWS!

Louisiana is the only state whose legal system is a combination of common law (which the other states follow), and Spanish and French civil law. As if one legal system weren't enough!

NO SCHOOL!

In some Louisiana high schools, students get to stay home for the opening day of—wait for it—squirrel-hunting season! Maybe it's time to petition your principal . . .

EVERYONE LOVES ELLEN!

Ellen Degeneres, the comedian and talk-show host, hails from Metairie. Before hitting it big, she was a waitress, a vacuum-cleaner saleswoman, and an oyster shucker. Hilarious!

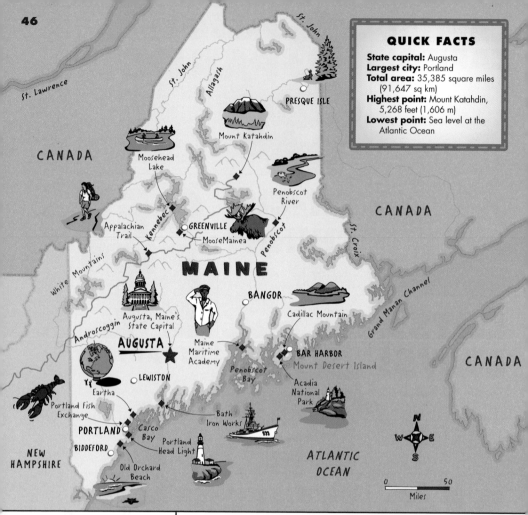

QUICK FACTS

State capital: Augusta
Largest city: Portland
Total area: 35,385 square miles (91,647 sq km)
Highest point: Mount Katahdin, 5,268 feet (1,606 m)
Lowest point: Sea level at the Atlantic Ocean

St. Lawrence

CANADA

St. John

Allagash

PRESQUE ISLE

Mount Katahdin

Moosehead Lake

Penobscot River

CANADA

Appalachian Trail

Kennebec

GREENVILLE

MooseMainea

Penobscot

St. Croix

MAINE

BANGOR

Grand Manan Channel

White Mountains

Androscoggin

Augusta, Maine's State Capital

Maine Maritime Academy

Cadillac Mountain

CANADA

AUGUSTA

LEWISTON

Eartha

Penobscot Bay

BAR HARBOR
Mount Desert Island

Acadia National Park

Portland Fish Exchange

Bath Iron Works

PORTLAND

Casco Bay

BIDDEFORD

Portland Head Light

Old Orchard Beach

ATLANTIC OCEAN

NEW HAMPSHIRE

N W E S

0   50
Miles

HALFWAY HAMLET

The town of Perry is on the 45th parallel. So what, you say? It's the halfway point between the equator and the North Pole! (Seriously! Go look at a globe!)

WHIRLPOOL WONDER

The largest whirlpool in the western hemisphere is the Old Sow, in Eastport. (No, it's not the kind of whirlpool you sit in with your friends. It's the natural kind!)

Ever heard the expression "She's got moxie"? It comes from Maine's state beverage, Moxie, a soft drink with spunk and pep, invented by Augustin Thompson of Union in 1876.

MAINE'S MOXIE!

TOP OF THE TRAIL

Baxter State Park in northern Maine, home of Mount Katahdin, is the beginning (or the end!) of the 2,178-mile-long Appalachian Trail, the longest marked footpath in America.

HOMETOWN HORROR HERO

Portland's Stephen King is known as the master of horror. He composes many of his tales in his Bangor home, which is surrounded by a cast iron fence featuring gargoyles!

AWESOME AUTHOR

North Brooklin's E. B. White wrote three children's classics that you are probably very familiar with: *Stuart Little*, *Charlotte's Web*, and *The Trumpet of the Swan*. (Don't know them? Go read one!)

In 1897, Louis Sockalexis of the Penobscot tribe of Maine became the first acknowledged Native American to play professional baseball.

A BASEBALL FIRST

THE "LOWLY" LOBSTER

Maine is famous for its lobster—people come from far and wide to eat it. But in colonial times lobster was so abundant, it was considered food for prisoners and servants!

OLDIE BUT GOODIE

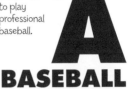

George Allen of Cherryfield patented a cool wrench in 1888 that can still be found in just about every workman's toolbox. What's it called? The Allen wrench, of course!

LAPTOPS FOR ALL!

In 2002, governor Angus King revolutionized public schools in Maine by giving every middle school student a laptop. The program has worked so well that it's still going.

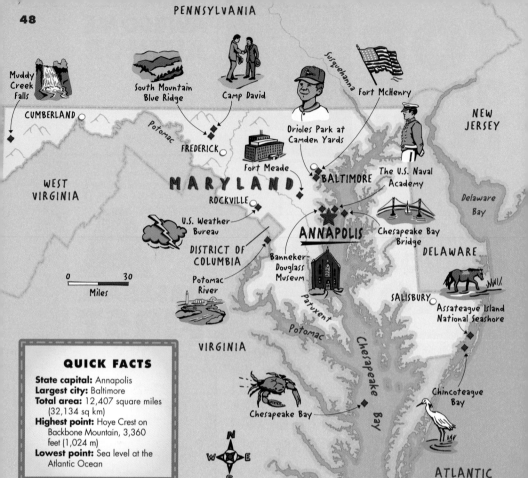

PENNSYLVANIA

Muddy Creek Falls

South Mountain Blue Ridge

Camp David

Susquehanna

Fort McHenry

CUMBERLAND

Potomac

FREDERICK

Orioles Park at Camden Yards

WEST VIRGINIA

Fort Meade

MARYLAND

BALTIMORE

The U.S. Naval Academy

NEW JERSEY

Delaware Bay

ROCKVILLE

U.S. Weather Bureau

DISTRICT OF COLUMBIA

ANNAPOLIS

Chesapeake Bay Bridge

DELAWARE

Banneker-Douglass Museum

Potomac River

SALISBURY

Assateague Island National Seashore

Patuxent

VIRGINIA

Potomac

Chesapeake Bay

Chincoteague Bay

QUICK FACTS

State capital: Annapolis
Largest city: Baltimore
Total area: 12,407 square miles (32,134 sq km)
Highest point: Hoye Crest on Backbone Mountain, 3,360 feet (1,024 m)
Lowest point: Sea level at the Atlantic Ocean

Chesapeake Bay

ATLANTIC OCEAN

N W E S

0   30
Miles

GRIDIRON POET

Famous Baltimore poet Edgar Allan Poe is held in high esteem by the National Football League! (Yes, the NFL.) The Baltimore Ravens are named after Poe's 1845 poem "The Raven."

BABE'S BASEBALL DESTINY

George Herman Ruth Sr., father of the legendary "Sultan of Swat," Babe Ruth, once ran Ruth's Cafe smack in the middle of what is now Oriole Park's center-field. Sounds like destiny!

OYSTER WARS

In the late 1800s, Maryland borrowed a cannon from the federal government to stop pirates who were after the oysters in Chesapeake Bay. (They must have been good oysters!)

CRUSTACEAN QUEEN

The National Hard Crab Derby is held every Labor Day weekend in Crisfield. It has crab races and cooking contests, and even crowns a Miss Crustacean every year!

COLOR COORDINATED

Maryland's state cat, the calico, shares three colors with the state flag, the state bird (the oriole), and the state butterfly (the checkerspot): orange, black, and white.

MEDIEVAL TIMES

Maryland's official sport is jousting! Competitors ride horses and carry a lance over an 80-yard course while trying to spear suspended rings. (At least they're not trying to spear each other.)

TIME KEEPER

Mathematician and astronomer Benjamin Banneker of Ellicott Mills designed and built America's first clock in 1753. It was made entirely out of wood and ran perfectly for over 30 years!

FISHERMAN LINGO

Maryland fishermen may sound like they're speaking a foreign language when they talk about jimmies, sooks, and busters, but they're really just talking about crabs!

LADY DAY

Billie Holiday, one of the world's greatest jazz singers, grew up in Baltimore. A statue of "Lady Day," as she was known, stands in Druid Hill.

CIVIL WAR SURVIVOR

The USS *Constellation*, docked in Baltimore's Inner Harbor, is the last surviving ship from the Civil War. The ship served America for 100 years and is now a museum.

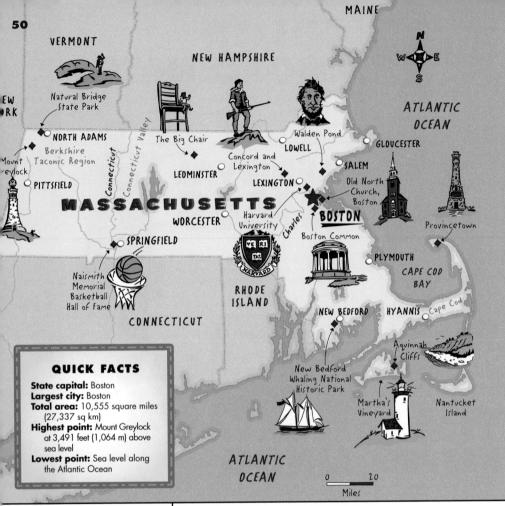

MAINE

VERMONT

NEW HAMPSHIRE

Natural Bridge
State Park

NEW YORK

ATLANTIC
OCEAN

The Big Chair

Walden Pond

LOWELL

GLOUCESTER

NORTH ADAMS

Berkshire
Taconic Region

Connecticut

Connecticut Valley

SALEM

Concord and
Lexington

Mount Greylock

LEOMINSTER

LEXINGTON

Old North
Church,
Boston

PITTSFIELD

MASSACHUSETTS

Harvard
University

Charles

BOSTON

WORCESTER

Provincetown

SPRINGFIELD

HARVARD VE RI TAS

Boston Common

PLYMOUTH

Naismith
Memorial
Basketball
Hall of Fame

RHODE
ISLAND

CAPE COD
BAY

CONNECTICUT

NEW BEDFORD

HYANNIS

Cape Cod

Aquinnah
Cliffs

New Bedford
Whaling National
Historic Park

Martha's
Vineyard

Nantucket
Island

QUICK FACTS

State capital: Boston
Largest city: Boston
Total area: 10,555 square miles
(27,337 sq km)
Highest point: Mount Greylock
at 3,491 feet (1,064 m) above
sea level
Lowest point: Sea level along
the Atlantic Ocean

ATLANTIC
OCEAN

0   20
Miles

TALENTED TRICKSTERS

The Massachusetts Institute of
Technology is famous for cranking out
geniuses—and for the crazy pranks
its geniuses pull off, like putting a fire
truck on the dome of a building.

WRITING ON THE WALL

In 1922 in Rockport, Swedish
immigrant Ellis Stenman built
a two-room house—and all its
furnishings—out of over 100,000
newspapers. Bet he never ran out
of things to read.

Lake Chargoggagoggmanchauggagoggchaubunagungamaugg, in Webster, has
the longest name in
American geography.
According to some
sources, it means, "You
fish on your side, I fish
on my side, and no one
fishes in the middle."

TRANSLATION, PLEASE?

CONSISTENT COOKING

SAM I AM

In 1812, Arlington's Samuel Wilson supplied the army with meat in containers stamped "U.S." Soldiers joked that "U.S." stood for Uncle Sam, and a great American symbol was born!

In 1896, Fannie Farmer of Medford published the first cookbook to use standard measurements such as the teaspoon and tablespoon—and it's still in print over 100 years later!

BABY SPOCK

Are you a *Star Trek* fan? Make a pilgrimage to Boston, where Leonard Nimoy—known to Trekkies as the half-Vulcan, half-human Spock—was born. Just watch out for the Vulcan nerve pinch!

Raytheon, a technology company in Waltham, created the first microwave in 1947. It was called a Radarange, it was as big as a refrigerator, and it cost between $2,000 and $3,000.

MICROWAVE MAGIC

DELICIOUS DISCOVERY

In 1930, Ruth Wakefield broke a chocolate bar into pieces for her cookie batter at the Toll House Inn in Whitman. The pieces didn't melt, and chocolate chips were born!

MOLASSES DISASTER

In 1919, a wave of molasses estimated at between 8 and 40 feet high flooded Boston's North End at 35 miles per hour after a tank containing 2.3 million gallons of the sticky stuff collapsed.

Clinton is home to the nation's oldest baseball diamond, which opened for play in 1878 and has hosted regular games of the great American pastime ever since!

FIRST FIELD

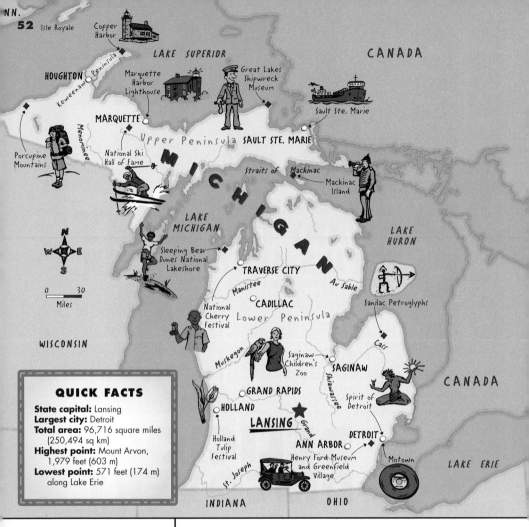

Copper Harbor

LAKE SUPERIOR

CANADA

HOUGHTON

Keweenaw Peninsula

Marquette Harbor Lighthouse

Great Lakes Shipwreck Museum

Sault Ste. Marie

MARQUETTE

Upper Peninsula   SAULT STE. MARIE

MICHIGAN

Menominee

Porcupine Mountains

National Ski Hall of Fame

Straits of   Mackinac

Mackinac Island

LAKE MICHIGAN

LAKE HURON

N W E S

0   30
Miles

Sleeping Bear Dunes National Lakeshore

Au Sable

Sanilac Petroglyphs

TRAVERSE CITY

Manistee

CADILLAC

Lower Peninsula

National Cherry Festival

WISCONSIN

Muskegon

Cass

Saginaw Children's Zoo

SAGINAW

Shiawassee

Spirit of Detroit

CANADA

GRAND RAPIDS

HOLLAND

LANSING

Grand

DETROIT

Holland Tulip Festival

ANN ARBOR

Henry Ford Museum and Greenfield Village

Motown

LAKE ERIE

St. Joseph

INDIANA   OHIO

QUICK FACTS

State capital: Lansing
Largest city: Detroit
Total area: 96,716 square miles (250,494 sq km)
Highest point: Mount Arvon, 1,979 feet (603 m)
Lowest point: 571 feet (174 m) along Lake Erie

MICHIGAN LOVES MADONNA

Madonna is a Michigan girl! The Queen of Pop was born in Bay City, and grew up in Rochester Hills. She left when she was 20, to pursue dancing in New York.

BRIDGE STATS

At 8,614 feet, the Mackinac Bridge is the longest suspension bridge in the western hemisphere. The bridge's deck is designed to move as much as 35 feet in high winds!

PENINSULA PARTY

Michigan's motto is, "If you seek a pleasant peninsula, look about you." Why? It's the only state with two peninsulas. (The Lower Peninsula looks like a giant mitten!)

SERIOUS ABOUT CEREAL

Important decisions about your breakfast cereal were probably made in Battle Creek, where, at one time, both Kellogg's and Post were headquartered. The companies were archrivals for years!

CREATIVE CAPITOL

The Michigan State Capitol building has more than nine acres of hand-painted surfaces! Designs include animals, flowers, trees, and even a mythical beast called a winged griffin.

ELVIS FEST!

The Michigan Elvis Fest in Ypsilanti is one of the largest tribute concerts in North America. The country's best Elvis impersonators honor the King in July, on the anniversary of his death.

LAKES APLENTY

Michigan has 11,000 lakes and 36,000 miles of streams. You can find water within 6 miles of wherever you are in the state! (Don't visit if you suffer from aquaphobia.)

SKIING HISTORY

We have Scandinavian immigrant miners and lumberjacks to thank for introducing skiing as a sport to the Ishpeming area, which is now home to the U.S. National Ski and Snowboard Hall of Fame.

MOTOWN MAN

Berry Gordy founded Motown Records in Detroit in 1959. It was the first music label owned by an African American to feature black artists who were popular across racial lines.

TREMENDOUS TIRE

Detroit has the world's largest tire, which started life as a Ferris wheel at the New York World's Fair in 1964. The 80-foot-tall, 12-ton tire has treads big enough to fit your head!

HOCKEY MANIA

Eveleth, home to the Hockey Hall of Fame, is known as the Capital of American Hockey because the city has contributed more professional players per capita than any other.

BRRRRRR!!!!

Embarrass is known as the nation's "Cold Spot." On February 2, 1996, Embarrass experienced one of lowest temperatures ever recorded in the Lower 48: -57°F!

MISSISSIPPI IN MINNESOTA

Lake Itasca, in Minnesota's Lake Itasca State Park, is the source—or starting point—for the mighty Mississippi River, once the country's most important transportation route.

ICE PALACE

The Saint Paul Winter Carnival, which is the oldest and largest winter festival in the nation, is reported to have featured an ice palace made of over 30,000 blocks of ice!

SUPER SHORES

Minnesota, "land of 10,000 lakes," has 90,000 miles of shoreline. That's more than California, Florida, and Hawai'i combined! (No wonder there's one boat for every six people in the state.)

MALL MANIA!

The Mall of America in Bloomington is the world's largest indoor shopping mall. An average of 11,000 people work in the mall, which is the size of 78 football fields!

BIG BUNYAN

Akeley may be small—the population hovers around 400—but it has a huge, 25-foot statue of Paul Bunyan. Go visit and sit in the mythological lumberjack's palm!

VIKING GRAFFITI

Some think that a runestone—an ancient stone with an inscription—found on a Douglas County farm, now in a museum in Alexandria, proves that the Vikings explored North America nearly 130 years before Christopher Columbus.

ALEXANDRIA BIRTHPLACE OF AMERICA

OVER THE RAINBOW

Grand Rapids is the birthplace of *The Wizard of Oz* star Judy Garland. If there's "no place like home," there must be no place like Grand Rapids!

HOT AIR

The Metrodome in Minneapolis is inflatable! It requires 250,000 cubic feet of air pressure per minute, and visitors use revolving doors to keep air from escaping.

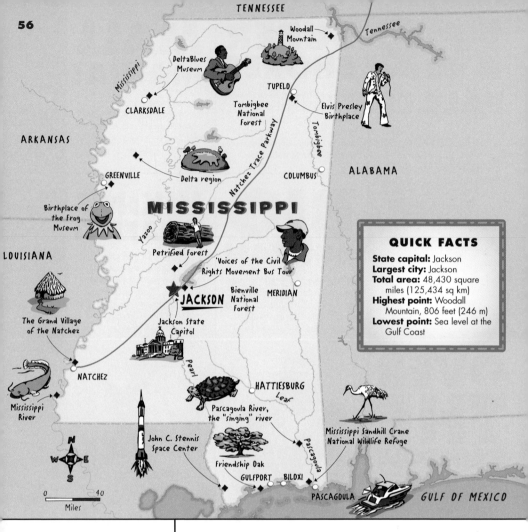

QUICK FACTS

State capital: Jackson
Largest city: Jackson
Total area: 48,430 square miles (125,434 sq km)
Highest point: Woodall Mountain, 806 feet (246 m)
Lowest point: Sea level at the Gulf Coast

Map labels: TENNESSEE, Woodall Mountain, Tennessee, DeltaBlues Museum, TUPELO, Elvis Presley Birthplace, CLARKSDALE, Tombigbee National Forest, Mississippi, ARKANSAS, GREENVILLE, Delta region, Natchez Trace Parkway, COLUMBUS, Tombigbee, ALABAMA, MISSISSIPPI, Birthplace of the Frog Museum, Yazoo, Petrified Forest, 'Voices of the Civil Rights Movement Bus Tour', LOUISIANA, JACKSON, Bienville National Forest, MERIDIAN, The Grand Village of the Natchez, Jackson State Capitol, Pearl, NATCHEZ, HATTIESBURG, Leaf, Mississippi River, Pascagoula River, the "singing" river, Mississippi Sandhill Crane National Wildlife Refuge, John C. Stennis Space Center, Friendship Oak, Pascagoula, GULFPORT, BILOXI, N W E S, 0 40 Miles, PASCAGOULA, GULF OF MEXICO

FLYING TURTLE

In the late 1880s, a gopher turtle completely encased in ice fell to the ground in Bovina during a May hailstorm. (Huh? Yeah. No one has any idea how this happened.)

LITERARY LEGEND

Eudora Welty of Jackson won every major prize for writing—except the Nobel Prize for Literature. She was originally a photographer, but literature won her heart and she never looked back.

FLOODED FOREST

The "Grand Canyon of Mississippi" is a 36-million-year-old petrified forest in Flora. The 100-foot-tall trees were swept away by a flood. (That must have been some flood!)

BIRTH OF B.B.

On September 16, 1925, Riley B. King was born in Itta Bena. In 1949, he changed his name to B.B. King—B.B. for "Blues Boy"—and quickly became a blues legend.

CITIZEN REBEL

Mississippi resident Jefferson Davis had his citizenship revoked in 1861, when he became the Confederate President. It was restored by President Jimmy Carter in 1978, 89 years after Davis died.

FIT FOR A KING

In 1935, Elvis Presley was born in Tupelo. The "shotgun shack" where he was born is part of the Elvis Presley Museum, which brings in $46 million a year!

SHOE REVOLUTION

In 1884, Phil Gilbert's Shoe Parlor in Vicksburg made history when it started selling pairs of shoes in boxes. Prior to that, shoes were sold individually. (Weird, right?!)

29 USA

ROCK & ROLL SINGER, 1935-1977

ELVIS PRESLEY

TOY HISTORY

President Theodore Roosevelt was hunting near Onward when he refused to shoot a helpless bear. A toy merchant then honored the kind president with a stuffed animal named "Teddy's Bear."

CREATION OF KERMIT

Jim Henson grew up playing on the banks of Deer Creek in Leland. Deer Creek is said to be the birthplace of his first Muppet invention, Kermit the Frog.

WHAT'S IN A NAME?

Mississippi is named for the mighty river that flows through it. The name comes from the Chippewa Indian words *mici zipi*, which mean "great river."

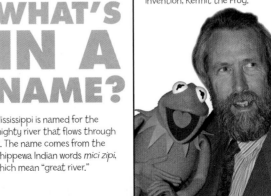

MISSISSIPPI THE MAGNOLIA STATE

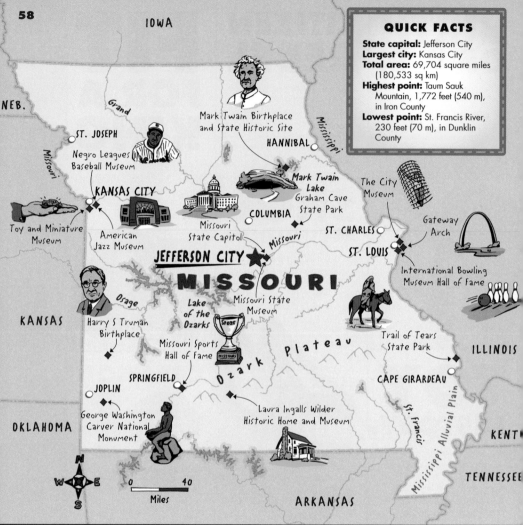

IOWA

NEB.

Grand

ST. JOSEPH

Negro Leagues
Baseball Museum

Missouri

KANSAS CITY

Toy and Miniature
Museum

American
Jazz Museum

Mark Twain Birthplace
and State Historic Site

HANNIBAL

Mississippi

Mark Twain
Lake
Graham Cave
State Park

The City
Museum

COLUMBIA

Missouri
State Capitol

JEFFERSON CITY ★

MISSOURI

Missouri

ST. CHARLES

Gateway
Arch

ST. LOUIS

International Bowling
Museum Hall of Fame

KANSAS

Osage

Harry S Truman
Birthplace

Lake
of the
Ozarks

Missouri State
Museum

Missouri Sports
Hall of Fame

Plateau

Trail of Tears
State Park

ILLINOIS

SPRINGFIELD

Ozark

CAPE GIRARDEAU

JOPLIN

George Washington
Carver National
Monument

Laura Ingalls Wilder
Historic Home and Museum

Mississippi Alluvial Plain

St. Francis

KENT

OKLAHOMA

TENNESSEE

N
W   E
S

0   40
Miles

ARKANSAS

QUICK FACTS

State capital: Jefferson City
Largest city: Kansas City
Total area: 69,704 square miles
(180,533 sq km)
Highest point: Taum Sauk
Mountain, 1,772 feet (540 m),
in Iron County
Lowest point: St. Francis River,
230 feet (70 m), in Dunklin
County

STEAMBOAT GRAVE

In 1856, the steamboat *Arabia* sank in the Missouri River. In 1988, excavators found it in a cornfield, a half mile away from the river and 45 feet underground!

DELICIOUS DEBUT!

Ice cream cones and iced tea had their debut at the St. Louis World's Fair in 1904. Let's all take a moment now to say a proper thank you!

MISSOURI MONIKER

Hannibal steamboat pilot Samuel Clemens—aka Mark Twain—took his pen name from the boatman's cry, "By the mark twain!" which alerted pilots to shallow water on the Mississippi.

George Washington Carver

32 USA

AWESOME ARCH

At 630 feet, the Jefferson National Memorial, also known as the Gateway Arch, is twice the height of the Statue of Liberty. It's America's tallest national monument!

MAIN STREET MODEL

Walt Disney lived in Marceline as a boy and loved the quintessential small town so much that he used it as the model for Disneyland's Main Street, USA.

PEANUT MAGIC

Chemist George Washington Carver, born near Diamond, revitalized the South's economy and changed agricultural practices and diet with his discovery that growing peanuts could improve soil quality.

FOUNTAIN CITY

Kansas City has more fountains than any other city in the world, except Rome, Italy. The first fountains were originally built to provide clean drinking water for animals.

MAN-MADE PARADISE

Bonne Terre is home to a former lead mine that was flooded with billions of gallons of water and turned into the world's largest underground resort for diving.

GREATEST THING SINCE . . .

The Chillicothe Baking Company sold the first loaf of sliced bread in 1928, thanks to the newly invented bread slicer. In 2007, Chillicothe officially became the "Home of Sliced Bread."

In 1811, New Madrid experienced an earthquake of such severity that parts of the Mississippi River actually flowed backward!

CRAZY CURRENT

MISSOURI

THE SHOW ME STATE

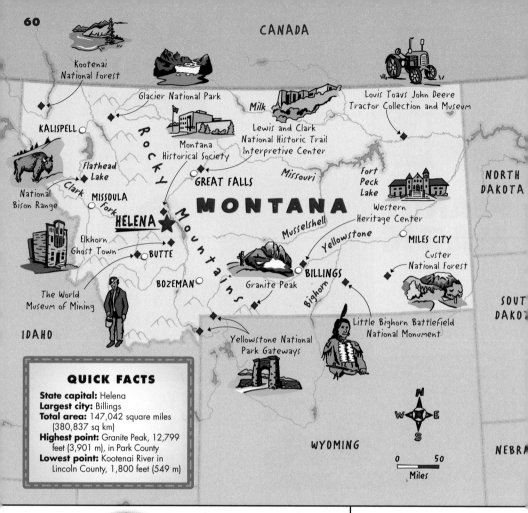

CANADA

Kootenai
National Forest

Glacier National Park

Milk

Louis Toavs John Deere
Tractor Collection and Museum

KALISPELL

Montana
Historical Society

Lewis and Clark
National Historic Trail
Interpretive Center

NORTH
DAKOTA

Flathead
Lake

Clark

MISSOULA

fork

HELENA

Missouri

GREAT FALLS

MONTANA

Fort
Peck
Lake

Western
Heritage Center

National
Bison Range

Elkhorn
Ghost Town

BUTTE

Musselshell

Yellowstone

MILES CITY

Custer
National Forest

The World
Museum of Mining

BOZEMAN

Granite Peak

BILLINGS

Bighorn

SOUT
DAKOT

IDAHO

Yellowstone National
Park Gateways

Little Bighorn Battlefield
National Monument

WYOMING

NEBR

QUICK FACTS

State capital: Helena
Largest city: Billings
Total area: 147,042 square miles
(380,837 sq km)
Highest point: Granite Peak, 12,799
feet (3,901 m), in Park County
Lowest point: Kootenai River in
Lincoln County, 1,800 feet (549 m)

N
W   E
S

0   50
Miles

BONE
BREAKTHROUGH

In 1978, a rock shop owner found a group of baby
dinosaur bones near Choteau. The site, now called
Egg Mountain, is rich in fossilized dinosaur eggs and
baby skeletons.

WOMAN
FOR
PEACE

In 1917, Missoula's Jeanette Rankin
became the first woman to serve in
Congress. She also holds the distinction of being the only representative
to vote against U.S. involvement in
World War II.

WORLD RECORD

Thanks to elementary school kids in Great Falls, the 201-foot-long Roe River was
listed in the *Guinness Book of World Records* as the shortest river in the world!

FROM FREEZING TO FINE

Loma holds the record for the greatest temperature change in a single day. On January 14-15, 1972, the temperature went from -59°F to 49°F!

DRAGON DRAMA

Christopher Paolini, the teenage author of *Eragon*, grew up in Paradise Valley. The natural beauty surrounding him—including mountains called the Crazies—inspired the dramatic settings in his books.

SIGN HERE!

When William Clark carved his signature and the date—July 25, 1806—into a rock at Pompeys Pillar, he left the only known physical evidence of Lewis and Clark's expedition.

GOLD RUSH MILLIONAIRES

In 1888, Helena had more millionaires per capita than any other city in the world. About $3.6 billion worth of the sparkly stuff was mined in the area during the gold rush.

WHERE GUSH THE GEYSERS

OREGON SHORT LINE
ALL RAIL ROUTE TO THE
YELLOWSTONE

According to the NPS, Yellowstone Park has 300 geysers. No, not geezers—geysers! Geysers are hot springs that erupt. The park, also known as Geyserland, is home to two-thirds of the world's spouting springs.

GREAT GEYSERLAND

GRAND SLAM!

The only pitcher ever to hit a grand slam in the World Series is Dave McNally from Billings. The Baltimore Oriole made history in 1970, against the Cincinnati Reds.

RUN, DOGS, RUN!

The Race to the Sky covers hundreds of miles. Mushers follow trails through wilderness areas and climb to an altitude of 6,000 feet. The race starts with a vet check, to make sure the dogs are ready to dash.

SOUTH DAKOTA

MINNESOTA

WYOMING

Toadstool Park

Badlands

Sandhills   Sand Hills

SCOTTSBLUFF   Chimney
Rock

North Platte

Oregon
Trail

Panorama
Point   South Platte

COLORADO

Niobrara

Nebraska
National
Forest

Lewis and Clark
Campsite

Missouri

NIOBRARA

IOWA

NEBRASKA

College Baseball
World Series

Loup

Platte

Nebraska
State Capitol

OMAHA

Missouri

Lake McConaughy

Great Platte River Road
Archway Monument

KEARNEY

GRAND ISLAND

LINCOLN

Henry
Doorly
Zoo

Republican

Harold Warp
Pioneer Village

Platte River

BEATRICE

Homestead National
Monument of America

KANSAS

N
W   E
S

0   50
Miles

QUICK FACTS

State capital: Lincoln
Largest city: Omaha
Total area: 77,354 square miles (200,347
  sq km)
Highest point: Panorama Point, 5,424 feet
  (1,653 m), located in Kimball County
Lowest point: Missouri River at 840 feet
  (256 m) in Richardson County

CRANE-I-NESS!

From February to April, thousands of tourists travel to the Platte River to watch a half million Sandhill cranes nest, feed, and store up energy for their migration.

CAR ART

Heard of Stonehenge, that cool arrangement of ancient stone slabs in England? Well, how about Carhenge? Alliance has an homage to Stonehenge made out of upended cars.

DIFFERENT STROKES

Nebraska is the only state with a unicameral legislature, meaning that it has only one house of government, the senate. All other states have both the house and the senate.

POWERFUL RESISTANCE

Red Cloud, a Lakota Indian born near North Platte in 1822, devoted his life to resisting conquest by the U.S. government, using both peaceful and violent methods.

FATHER OF THE RODEO

The performer Buffalo Bill Cody started his "Buffalo Bill's Wild West" show in North Platte in 1883, hiring real cowboys and cowgirls to demonstrate bronco riding and roping.

THE LIBERTY SWING

Hebron's claim to fame is a giant "porch" swing made for the town's 4th of July celebration that can hold up to 16 adults—or 32 kids—at one time.

ALL HAIL!

On June 22, 2003, a giant-sized hailstone fell in Aurora during a thunderstorm. Thanks to quick-thinking locals, the record-breaking ice ball was preserved—in a freezer, of course.

"HEY, KIDS!"

Edwin Perkins of Hastings invented Kool-Ade (now Kool-Aid)—earlier called Fruit Smack—in 1927. By 1950, his company was producing nearly a million packets of Kool-Aid a day!

SMALL HALL

Maskell is home to the nation's smallest city hall. How small is "smallest," you ask? Pretty small! About 10 feet by 10 feet. (Hopefully Maskell's mayor is small, too.)

YAKITY YAK

Nebraska has one of North America's greatest herds of yak, a big, wooly creature that looks like a bull and is normally found in the Himalayas in Asia.

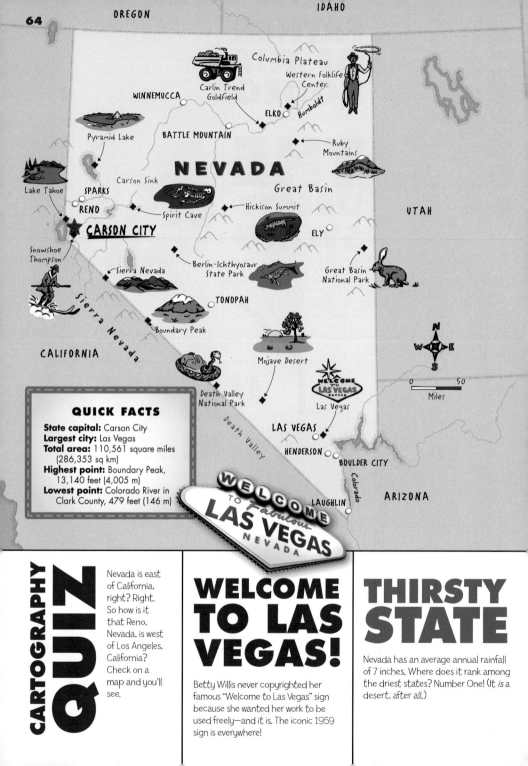

OREGON

IDAHO

Columbia Plateau

Western Folklife Center

Carlin Trend Goldfield

WINNEMUCCA

ELKO

Humboldt

Pyramid Lake

BATTLE MOUNTAIN

Ruby Mountains

NEVADA

Great Basin

Carson Sink

Lake Tahoe

SPARKS

RENO

UTAH

Hickison Summit

Spirit Cave

CARSON CITY

ELY

Snowshoe Thompson

Berlin-Ichthyosaur State Park

Great Basin National Park

Sierra Nevada

TONOPAH

CALIFORNIA

Sierra Nevada

Boundary Peak

Mojave Desert

N
W   E
S

0   50
Miles

Death Valley National Park

WELCOME TO LAS VEGAS NEVADA

Las Vegas

LAS VEGAS

Death Valley

HENDERSON

BOULDER CITY

Colorado

ARIZONA

LAUGHLIN

QUICK FACTS

State capital: Carson City
Largest city: Las Vegas
Total area: 110,561 square miles
(286,353 sq km)
Highest point: Boundary Peak,
13,140 feet (4,005 m)
Lowest point: Colorado River in
Clark County, 479 feet (146 m)

WELCOME TO Fabulous LAS VEGAS NEVADA

CARTOGRAPHY QUIZ

Nevada is east of California, right? Right. So how is it that Reno, Nevada, is west of Los Angeles, California? Check on a map and you'll see.

WELCOME TO LAS VEGAS!

Betty Willis never copyrighted her famous "Welcome to Las Vegas" sign because she wanted her work to be used freely—and it is. The iconic 1959 sign is everywhere!

THIRSTY STATE

Nevada has an average annual rainfall of 7 inches. Where does it rank among the driest states? Number One! (It *is* a desert, after all.)

DESERTED DESERT TOWN

The population of Survival Town is. . . zero! The federal government built the city—complete with houses and offices—in the desert to test the effects of a nuclear explosion in 1955.

BURNING MAN

Every year, thousands journey to the Black Rock Desert to participate in an intense, week-long art festival called Burning Man, which culminates in the burning of a giant "man" sculpture.

Lake Tahoe, in the Sierra Nevada mountains, is the largest, highest alpine lake in North America. It's pretty old, too—it was formed about 2 million years ago!

WAY UP THERE

READY, SET . . . CAMEL!

Virginia City hosts the International Camel Races every year, despite the fact that the race originated as a joke in a newspaper in 1959.

Las Vegas's favorite son, Andre Agassi, was one of the world's greatest tennis players before he retired in 2006. He won eight grand slams and an Olympic medal.

GOLDEN STATE

Elko hosts the nation's biggest open-pit gold mine, called Goldstrike. Nevada produces more gold than any other state. No wonder people go there to strike it rich!

ANDRE THE GREAT

COSTLY COMMUNIQUÉ!

In order to meet the deadline for statehood in 1864, Nevada sent its entire constitution to Washington, D.C., by telegraph. The telegraph cost $3,400—that's nearly $47,000 by today's standards!

CANADA

PACIFIC OCEAN

Space Needle
SEATTLE
OLYMPIA ★ **WASHINGTON**
Mount Rainier
National Park

SALEM ★ Mount Hood
OREGON
Wild Horses
of Oregon
Crater Lake
National Park

Glacier
National Park
HELENA ★ **MONTANA**
Little Bighorn Battlefield
National Monument

National State
Bison Range

Craters of the Moon
National Monument
BOISE ★ **IDAHO**
Lewis and Clark
National Historic Trail

Yellowstone
National Park
WYOMING
Independence
Rock
CHEYENNE ★

Geographical Center
North America
★ BISMARCK
NORTH DAKOTA
World's Largest Bison
Corn Palace
SOUTH DAKOTA
★ PIERRE
Mount Rushmore
National Memorial

Lassen Volcanic
National Park
Fisherman's
Wharf
SACRAMENTO ★
SAN FRANCISCO

Ruby Mountains
Lake Tahoe
CARSON CITY ★ **NEVADA**
Marshall Gold
Discovery State
Historic Park

GREAT
SALT
LAKE
★ SALT LAKE CITY
Dinosaur
National
Monument
UTAH
Rainbow Bridge
National Monument

Pikes Peak in the
Rocky Mountains
DENVER ★
COLORADO
Colorado River

Chimney Rock National
Historic Site
NEBRASKA
Prairie Dog Towns

Tallgrass
Prairie
KANSAS
ROUTE
66

CALIFORNIA
Hollywood
OSCAR
LOS ANGELES
WELCOME
LAS VEGAS
Las Vegas
Joshua Tree
National Park

Sea World

Four Corners
Monument
Grand Canyon
National Park
ARIZONA
PHOENIX ★
Sonoran
Desert

Carlsbad Caverns
SANTA FE ★
NEW MEXICO
Taos Pueblo

Odessa Meteor Crater

Longhorn
Ranching
OKLAHOMA
OKLAHOMA
Nat
Ha

World
Cow
TEXAS
The Alamo
AUS
Lyndon
Space

MEXICO

ALASKA
Trans-Alaska
Pipeline
Mount McKinley
(Denali)   ANCHORAGE
CANADA
JUNEAU
PACIFIC
OCEAN

PACIFIC OCEAN
HONOLULU ★
HAWAI'I
Hawai'i Volcanoes
National Park

Rio Grande

Land of 10,000 Lakes
LAKE SUPERIOR
CANADA
MAINE
Moose Country
Lobster Harvesting
AUGUSTA ★
NESOTA
Copper Harbor
VT.
N.H.
The Big Chair
Vermont Maple Syrup
★ MONTPELIER
SAINT PAUL ★
MINNEAPOLIS
WISCONSIN
Ox
LAKE HURON
Empire Apples
NEW YORK
ALBANY ★ CONCORD ★ BOSTON ★
Mississippi River
Sleeping Bear Dunes National Lakeshore
MICHIGAN
MASS.
CONN.
Racine Reef Lighthouse
MADISON ★
LANSING ★ DETROIT ★
New York City
PROVIDENCE ★
R.I.
HARTFORD ★
Mounds Monument
LAKE ONTARIO
Newport
Long Island Sound
IOWA
CHICAGO
LAKE ERIE
Carnegie Museums
NEW YORK
DES MOINES ★
Sears Tower
Corn Belt
Rock and Roll Hall of Fame and Museum
PENNSYLVANIA
Statue of Liberty
HARRISBURG ★
TRENTON ★
Statue of Liberty
ILLINOIS
INDIANA
OHIO
Edison National Historic Site
George Washington Carver National Monument
Lincoln Home
SPRINGFIELD
INDIANAPOLIS
COLUMBUS ★
Liberty Bell
N.J.
Mound City Group National Monument
MD.
ANNAPOLIS ★
DEL.
JEFFERSON CITY ★
SAINT LOUIS ★
Cahokia Mounds
Indianapolis Motor Speedway
WEST VIRGINIA
WASHINGTON, DC ★
Fenwick Lighthouse
MISSOURI
FRANKFORT ★
West Virginia Coal Miner
Monticello
RICHMOND ★
Gateway Arch
River
Fort Knox
CHARLESTON ★
VIRGINIA
Chesapeake Bay
KENTUCKY
Churchill Downs
Great Smoky Mountains National Park
RALEIGH ★
NASHVILLE ★
NORTH CAROLINA
ARKANSAS
TENNESSEE
Nashville Music
Cape Hatteras
LITTLE ROCK ★
City of Atlanta
SOUTH CAROLINA
Birthplace of Elvis Presley
Moundville
COLUMBIA ★
Hot Springs
ATLANTA ★
Cypress Gardens
MISSISSIPPI
ALABAMA
GEORGIA
JACKSON ★
MONTGOMERY ★
Tuskegee Institute
Peach Growing
Crawfish
Pascagoula River
Dauphin Island Sea Lab
LOUISIANA
BATON ROUGE ★
TALLAHASSEE ★
Mardi Gras New Orleans
Gulf Islands National Seashore
FLORIDA
John F. Kennedy Space Center
GULF OF MEXICO
Everglades National Park
MIAMI
N
W ★ E
S

ATLANTIC OCEAN

San Cristobal
SAN JUAN
PUERTO RICO
Tres Picachos
CARIBBEAN SEA

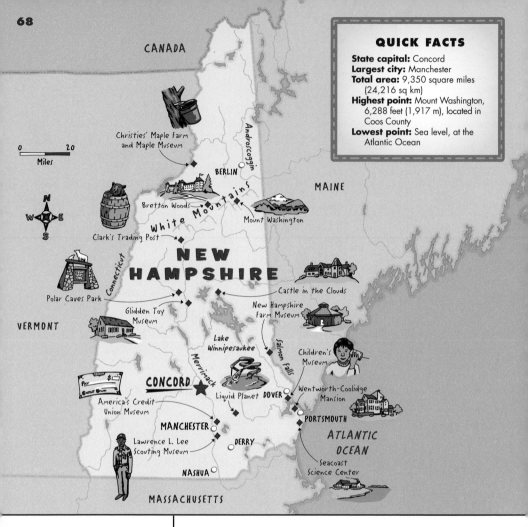

CANADA

QUICK FACTS

State capital: Concord
Largest city: Manchester
Total area: 9,350 square miles (24,216 sq km)
Highest point: Mount Washington, 6,288 feet (1,917 m), located in Coos County
Lowest point: Sea level, at the Atlantic Ocean

Christies' Maple Farm and Maple Museum

BERLIN

Androscoggin

MAINE

0   20
Miles

N
W   E
S

Bretton Woods   White Mountains

Mount Washington

Clark's Trading Post

NEW HAMPSHIRE

Connecticut

Polar Caves Park

Glidden Toy Museum

Castle in the Clouds

New Hampshire Farm Museum

VERMONT

Lake Winnipesaukee

Salmon Falls

Children's Museum

Merrimack

CONCORD

Liquid Planet   DOVER

Wentworth-Coolidge Mansion

PAY $

America's Credit Union Museum

PORTSMOUTH

MANCHESTER

ATLANTIC OCEAN

Lawrence L. Lee Scouting Museum

DERRY

Seacoast Science Center

NASHUA

MASSACHUSETTS

BRILLIANT BEARS

Want to see a bear eat ice cream? Visit Clark's Trading Post in Lincoln, where daily bear shows involve "bearsketball," balancing acts, and drinking out of "bear cans."

ANCIENT ARTS

Want to learn how to be a blacksmith or a cooper? Apply to New Hampshire's Traditional Arts apprentice program and keep the old arts alive by learning from a master.

REPUBLICAN REBELS

In 1853, in Exeter, Amos Tuck called a secret meeting of politicians who were opposed to the Democrats, suggesting they form their own party, the Republicans. And so it began!

TRAVELING IN STYLE

In 1938, the first tramway was built, carrying people to the top of Cannon Mountain in Franconia Notch. Nearly 7 million people rode it before it was replaced in 1980.

RISE AND SHINE

Levi Hutchins of Concord was the first American to be woken up by an alarm clock, which he invented in 1787. School kids everywhere can thank Levi (or not).

TALL AND BLUSTERY

Mount Washington is the highest peak in the northeast. It is 6,288 feet and holds the record for the highest wind gust recorded on the earth's surface: 231 mph!

General John Stark of Londonderry penned New Hampshire's motto, "Live free or die." But that's only half of what he wrote. The rest is, "Death is not the worst of evils."

EXTREME MOTTO

PLACE OF PEACE

President Theodore Roosevelt won a Nobel Peace Prize for bringing Russia and Japan together in Portsmouth to sign the Treaty of Portsmouth in 1905, which ended the Russo-Japanese war.

PLASTICS GENIUS

Earl Tupper of Berlin invented an extremely popular food storage system and started his company in 1938. Can you guess what he invented? (Hint: check out his last name!) Yup—Tupperware!

COTTON GIANT

The Amoskeag Manufacturing Company in Manchester was the largest cotton textile mill in the world in the early 20th century. The mill made cloth for just about everything—even Levi's jeans!

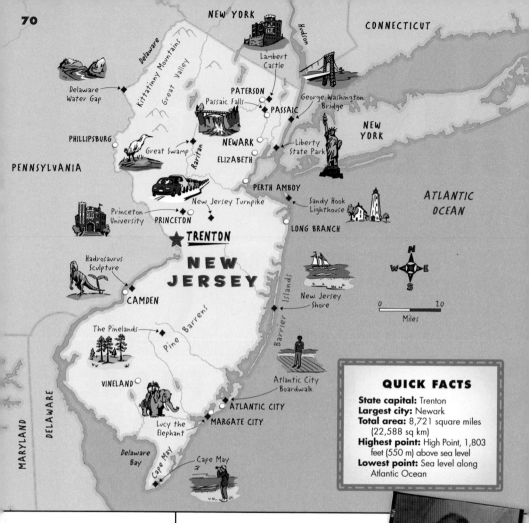

NEW YORK

CONNECTICUT

Delaware

Kittatinny Mountains

Great Valley

Hudson

Lambert Castle

Delaware Water Gap

PATERSON

Passaic Falls

PASSAIC

George Washington Bridge

PHILLIPSBURG

Great Swamp

Raritan

NEWARK

ELIZABETH

Liberty State Park

NEW YORK

PENNSYLVANIA

New Jersey Turnpike

PERTH AMBOY

Sandy Hook Lighthouse

ATLANTIC OCEAN

Princeton University

PRINCETON

LONG BRANCH

★ TRENTON

N E W
J E R S E Y

N
W E
S

Hadrosaurus Sculpture

CAMDEN

New Jersey Shore

0   20
Miles

The Pinelands

Pine Barrens

Barrier Islands

VINELAND

Atlantic City Boardwalk

QUICK FACTS

State capital: Trenton
Largest city: Newark
Total area: 8,721 square miles (22,588 sq km)
Highest point: High Point, 1,803 feet (550 m) above sea level
Lowest point: Sea level along Atlantic Ocean

Lucy the Elephant

ATLANTIC CITY

MARGATE CITY

MARYLAND

DELAWARE

Delaware Bay

Cape May

Cape May

When Thomas Edison invented the phonograph in 1877 in Menlo Park, he tested it by recording—and playing back—"Mary Had a Little Lamb."

EDISON GOLD MOULD RECORD

TESTING, TESTING

FORCEFUL PHOTOS

Dorothea Lange, one of the country's most important photographers, was born in Hoboken. Lange is famous for her striking Depression-era photos of farmers and migrant workers.

HIGHEST LAND

The appropriately named Highlands has the—wait for it—highest elevation of any coastal city from Texas to Maine. It's 226 feet above sea level. You should see the view!

SUBMARINE SUCCESS

John Holland built the first successful submarine in 1900 in Elizabethport. He sold it to the Navy for $150,000 and they named it the USS *Holland*, in his honor.

DINER DENSITY

New Jersey has one of the highest population densities in the country: about 1,175 people per square mile. Maybe that's why the state also has the most diners in the world!

EPIC POEM

William Carlos Williams, a great American poet and a doctor from Rutherford, wrote an epic poem called *Paterson*, about the industrial city. It was originally over five books long!

HUT, HUT, HIKE!

The first college football game was played in New Brunswick between the College of New Jersey (now known as Princeton) and Rutgers College (now known as Rutgers University) in 1869.

A TELLING TITLE

The New Jersey seaport Elizabeth calls itself "America's Containership Capital." With a reported 23 cranes, 1 million square feet of storage space, and its own on-dock railroad system, it's earned that title!

DEMANDING THE VOTE

Suffragette Alice Paul of Mount Laurel was jailed for demonstrating at the White House in 1917. Prison doctors tried to have her declared insane in order to discredit her.

SECRETS OF THE GAME

Charles Darrow, the inventor of Monopoly, spent his summers in Atlantic City. He loved the city so much, he borrowed its street names for his game!

Aztec Ruins National Monument

COLORADO

KANSAS

Rocky Mountains

San Juan

OKLAHOMA

FARMINGTON

Rocky Mountains

Sangre de Cristo Mountains

Colorado Plateau

Chaco Culture National Historical Park

TAOS

Sangre de Cristo Mountains

SANTA FE

LAS VEGAS

Palace of the Governors

GALLUP

Petroglyph National Monument

Canadian

N
W E
S

0 40
Miles

ALBUQUERQUE

National Hispanic Cultural Center

University of New Mexico

Rio Grande

NEW MEXICO

Pecos River

TEXAS

Western Heritage Museum

ROSWELL

Pecos

White Sands National Monument

Gila

Gila National Forest

Carlsbad Caverns National Park

Rio Grande

LAS CRUCES

QUICK FACTS

State capital: Santa Fe
Largest city: Albuquerque
Total area: 121,590 square miles (314,918 sq km)
Highest point: Wheeler Peak, 13,161 feet (4,011 m)
Lowest point: Red Bluff Reservoir, 2,842 feet (866 m)

MEXICO

TEXAS

POLITICAL PARADE

In 1871, Democrats and Republicans paraded through Mesilla, and things got violent. The ensuing fight became known as the "Battle of the Bands." because both parties had marching bands!

INSPIRATION IN ALBUQUERQUE

In 1975. Bill Gates took a leave of absence from Harvard to work at a company in Albuquerque that had just built the first microcomputer. A year later, he trademarked Microsoft.

SANTA FE'S STATURE

Santa Fe has the highest elevation of any state capital—it's 7,000 feet above sea level. The highest point in the city is the capitol building, which is pretty appropriate!

"ONLY YOU!"

One of America's great celebrities got his start when he was rescued from a fire in Lincoln National Forest as a youngster in 1950. Who was it? Smokey Bear!

PREVENT SMOKEY FOREST FIRES

PARCHED PAVEMENT

Reportedly only one quarter of New Mexico's roads are paved. The climate is so dry that the parched earth creates "pavement" that's just as good as the real stuff!

BEEP, BEEP!

At 15 miles per hour, New Mexico's state bird, the roadrunner, is one of the fastest birds on the ground. It can catch—and eat—rattlesnakes, rodents, and scorpions!

DYNAMIC DUCKS

Deming hosts the annual Great American Duck Race. There are duck parades and pageants, tortilla tosses, spicy chili cook-offs, and even a crowning of a duck queen!

ALIEN INCIDENT

Interested in aliens? Roswell is your town! Visit the International UFO Museum and Research Center to learn about the 1947 "Roswell Incident," when a UFO reportedly crashed near the town.

PARDON THE INTERRUPTION

The government took over Los Alamos in 1947 for atomic research. The town began self-governance again in 1962, and the Los Alamos National Laboratory became a national historic landmark.

FLAG FACTS

New Mexico's flag sports an ancient sun symbol created by a Native America people called the Zia. The four sections symbolize the four main directions, the seasons, the parts of the day, and stages of life.

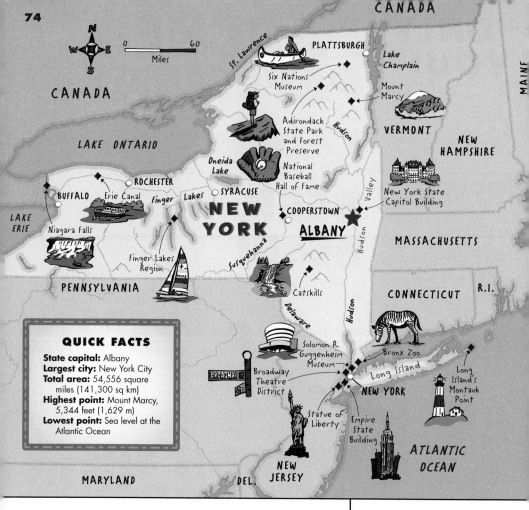

QUICK FACTS

State capital: Albany
Largest city: New York City
Total area: 54,556 square miles (141,300 sq km)
Highest point: Mount Marcy, 5,344 feet (1,629 m)
Lowest point: Sea level at the Atlantic Ocean

CANAL CELEBRATION

In 1825, "word" of the Erie Canal's completion traveled over 350 miles from Buffalo to New York City in just 81 minutes. How? The sounds of shots from cannons placed along the canal!

NYACK'S NIGHTHAWK

Edward Hopper, the artist behind the 1942 painting Nighthawks, hailed from Nyack. The haunting painting of customers in a diner late at night was inspired by an eatery in Manhattan.

AMERICA'S DESSERT

Pearle Wait, a carpenter in LeRoy, revolutionized American desserts in 1897 by adding fruit flavoring to gelatin while trying to make cough medicine. His wife named the jiggly stuff Jell-O.

BASEBALL BALONEY!

The Baseball Hall of Fame is located in Cooperstown, where Abner Doubleday was once rumored to have invented the game in 1839—even though he never made such claims himself.

FOUNDING FATHER'S TABLOID

The *New York Post* is one of the country's oldest newspapers. It was founded by Alexander Hamilton in 1801 in New York City.

LONG TIME COMING

Suffragettes gathered in Seneca Falls in 1848 for the first women's rights convention, to discuss winning the right to vote. Seventy-two years later, that right was finally granted.

IN A JAM

In 1848, Niagara Falls stopped flowing for 30 hours! Why? Ice floes from Lake Erie had jammed and blocked the water headed to the falls.

HAMILTON

UNUSUAL INAUGURATION

George Washington was inaugurated in New York City—at the time, the nation's capital—in 1789. He is the only president in history to take the oath in the Big Apple!

BETHEL-STOCK?

Contrary to popular belief, the three-day music festival known as Woodstock did not take place in Woodstock. It happened in Bethel in 1969, and half a million people were there!

ELEPHANT CROSSING

In 1884, after the Brooklyn Bridge was finished, P.T. Barnum led 21 circus elephants—including Jumbo!—across it in order to prove to the public that the bridge was safe.

Twenty One Elephants
AND STILL STANDING

APRIL JONES PRINCE   FRANÇOIS ROCA

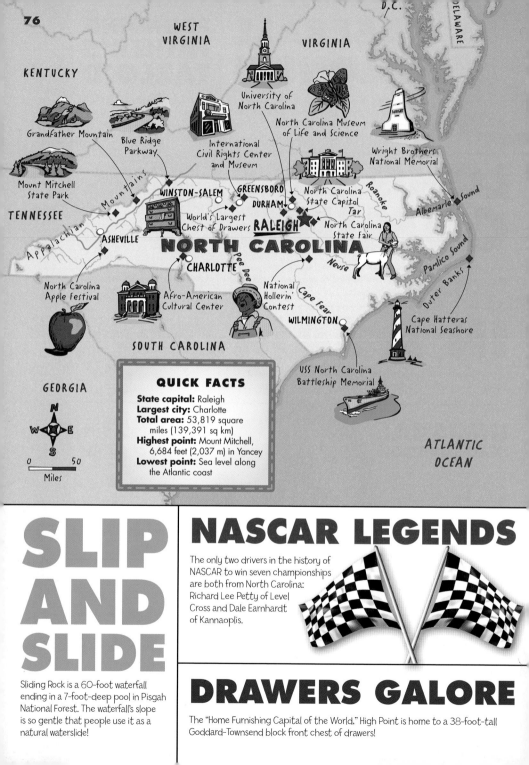

KENTUCKY

WEST VIRGINIA

VIRGINIA

D.C.

DELAWARE

TENNESSEE

Grandfather Mountain

Blue Ridge Parkway

Mount Mitchell State Park

University of North Carolina

International Civil Rights Center and Museum

North Carolina Museum of Life and Science

Wright Brothers National Memorial

North Carolina State Capitol

Albemarle Sound

Roanoke

WINSTON-SALEM

GREENSBORO

DURHAM

RALEIGH

World's Largest Chest of Drawers

NORTH CAROLINA

North Carolina State Fair

Tar

ASHEVILLE

Appalachian

Mountains

Pamlico Sound

Neuse

Outer Banks

Pee Dee

CHARLOTTE

North Carolina Apple Festival

Afro-American Cultural Center

National Hollerin' Contest

Cape Fear

WILMINGTON

Cape Hatteras National Seashore

SOUTH CAROLINA

GEORGIA

N W E S

0   50
Miles

QUICK FACTS

State capital: Raleigh
Largest city: Charlotte
Total area: 53,819 square miles (139,391 sq km)
Highest point: Mount Mitchell, 6,684 feet (2,037 m) in Yancey
Lowest point: Sea level along the Atlantic coast

USS North Carolina Battleship Memorial

ATLANTIC OCEAN

SLIP AND SLIDE

Sliding Rock is a 60-foot waterfall ending in a 7-foot-deep pool in Pisgah National Forest. The waterfall's slope is so gentle that people use it as a natural waterslide!

NASCAR LEGENDS

The only two drivers in the history of NASCAR to win seven championships are both from North Carolina: Richard Lee Petty of Level Cross and Dale Earnhardt of Kannaoplis.

DRAWERS GALORE

The "Home Furnishing Capital of the World," High Point is home to a 38-foot-tall Goddard-Townsend block front chest of drawers!

BLACKBEARD'S LAST SWIM

The pirate Blackbeard fought his last battle at Ocracoke in 1718. Legend says his headless body was thrown off a Naval ship, supposedly swimming around the ship three times before sinking!

PLANNING AHEAD

Chatham County is home to a military bunker several stories below ground, known as the Big Hole. Its purpose? To maintain communications in the event of a nuclear attack. (How cheerful—*not!*)

FANCY FORKS

At a typical 8-course dinner at the Biltmore House—the 250-room Vanderbilt mansion completed in 1895 in Asheville—guests used 15 different pieces of sterling silver utensils.

ART FOR ALL

In 1947, North Carolina became the first state to use public funds to purchase an art collection. You can see the collection at the North Carolina Museum of Art—for free!

DEMAND FOR DONUTS

When Vernon Rudolph started Krispy Kreme in 1937 in Old Salem, he had to cut a hole in the bakery wall to accommodate the many customers demanding his delicious donuts!

Even after he'd made it big, basketball great Michael Jordan of Wilmington used to wear his University of North Carolina shorts under his Chicago Bulls uniform for good luck.

SUPER SHORTS

DARE TO DISAPPEAR

In 1587, Virginia Dare of Roanoke became the first English child born in North America. But no one knows what happened to her or the other colonists. They simply disappeared.

NORTH CAROLINA THE TAR HEEL STATE

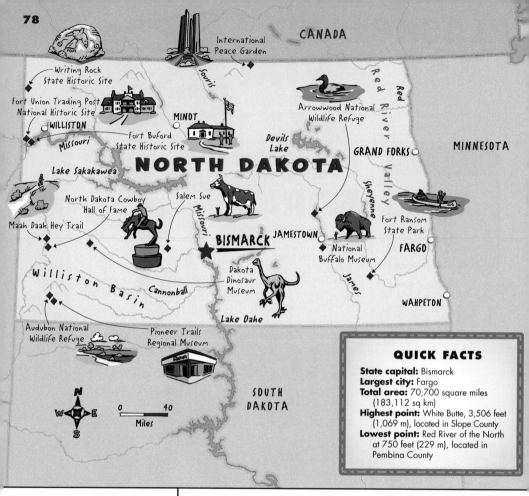

CANADA

International
Peace Garden

Writing Rock
State Historic Site

Fort Union Trading Post
National Historic Site

WILLISTON

Missouri

Fort Buford
State Historic Site

MINOT

Souris

Arrowwood National
Wildlife Refuge

Devils
Lake

Red River Valley

GRAND FORKS

MINNESOTA

Lake Sakakawea

NORTH DAKOTA

North Dakota Cowboy
Hall of Fame

Salem Sue

Maah Daah Hey Trail

Missouri

Sheyenne

Fort Ransom
State Park

FARGO

BISMARCK ★

JAMESTOWN

National
Buffalo Museum

Williston Basin

Cannonball

Dakota
Dinosaur
Museum

James

WAHPETON

Lake Oahe

Audubon National
Wildlife Refuge

Pioneer Trails
Regional Museum

Museum

SOUTH
DAKOTA

N
W E
S

0   40
Miles

QUICK FACTS

State capital: Bismarck
Largest city: Fargo
Total area: 70,700 square miles
(183,112 sq km)
Highest point: White Butte, 3,506 feet
(1,069 m), located in Slope County
Lowest point: Red River of the North
at 750 feet (229 m), located in
Pembina County

GOBBLE, GOBBLE

Every summer since the early 1960s, Aneta has hosted what they call the world's largest turkey barbeque. The event attracts thousands of people, and they barbeque close to 300 turkeys!

GIVE PEACE A CHANCE

The International Peace Garden straddles the boundary between North Dakota and the Canadian province of Manitoba. It features a floral clock and a memorial to those who lost their lives on 9/11.

TREMENDOUS TV ANTENNA

At 2,063 feet, the KVLY-TV Tower near Galesburg is the tallest structure in North America! (The only human-made structure that's taller is the Burj Dubai, in the United Arab Emirates.)

BUFFALO CITY

Jamestown, known as Buffalo City, has been home to a 26-foot-tall, 46-foot-long, 60-ton sculpture of a buffalo since 1959. It also has a (real!) albino buffalo named Dakota Miracle.

CENTRAL NORTH AMERICA

In 1931, Rugby was declared the geographical center of North America and honored with a pyramid-shaped monument. The town's unofficial motto is, fittingly, "Welcome to the center of it all!"

THE NAME GAME

In 1947, and again in 1989, the state legislature struck down a proposed resolution to strike the word "North" from North Dakota. For now, "Dakota" is just a nickname . . .

NORDIC CELEBRATION

Do not confuse the Horse Fest with Minot's Høstfest, North America's largest Scandinavian festival featuring Nordic cuisine (lutefisk, also known as fish in lye!) and clothing (clogs!).

GEOGRAPHICAL CENTER OF NORTH AMERICA
RUGBY, N.D.

CORNERSTONE CAFE
WELCOMES YOU TO RUGBY

A FLIGHT FIRST

In 1928, Carl Ben Eielson of Hatton was the first person to fly a plane across the Arctic Ocean. The flight took a grueling 20 hours!

UNFAIRLY NAMED!

Devils Lake was actually named Spirit Lake by the Sioux Indians, but white settlers mistranslated the name. The "evil" name stuck, owing to legends of monsters in the lake.

HORSING AROUND

The Taylor Horse Fest attracts close to 6,000 people each July and features just about every kind of horse event you can think of . . . including a Horse Fest musical!

CANADA

MICHIGAN

LAKE ERIE

Marblehead Lighthouse

TOLEDO

Maumee

Rock and Roll Hall of Fame

CLEVELAND

Cuyahoga

SANDUSKY

American Civil War Museum of Ohio

African Safari Wildlife Park

Sandusky

Cedar Point Amusement Park

AKRON

YOUNGSTOWN

PENNSYLVANIA

Edison Birthplace Museum

Neil Armstrong Air & Space Museum

CANTON

Pro Football Hall of Fame

Scioto

OHIO

INDIANA

Wyandot Popcorn Museum

Schoenbrunn Village State Memorial

Appalachian Plateau

N
W   E
S

SunWatch Indian Village/ Archaeological Park

Ohio Statehouse

Muskingum

Ohio

WEST VIRGINIA

0   30
Miles

DAYTON

The Horseshoe, Ohio State University

COLUMBUS

Great Miami

Scioto

Hocking Hills State Park

QUICK FACTS

State capital: Columbus
Largest city: Columbus
Total area: 44,825 square miles (116,096 sq km)
Highest point: Campbell Hill, 1,550 feet (472 m), located in Logan County
Lowest point: Ohio River, 455 feet (139 m), located in Hamilton County

Cincinnati Zoo & Botanical Garden

CINCINNATI

Ohio

KENTUCKY

A DRAWING DELIGHT

Bryan is home to the Ohio Art Company, which manufactures one of the most popular and creative toys invented in the 20th century—the Etch A Sketch!

EXTRAORDINARY ELECTION

Cleveland elected the first African American mayor of a major city in 1967. Carl B. Stokes became mayor after graduating from law school and serving three terms in the Ohio legislature.

ROLLER COASTER MANIA

Cedar Point Amusement Park in Sandusky has 17 roller coasters—that's more than any other park. Pay a visit and ride the Mean Streak, one of the steepest roller coasters in the world!

COWABUNGA!

Nancy Cartwright, the voice of Bart Simpson, was born in Kettering. Yes, you read that right—a woman provides the voice of *The Simpsons*'s famous fourth-grade troublemaker!

BIRTHPLACE OF PRESIDENTS

Seven U.S. presidents were born in Ohio! Ulysses Grant, Rutherford Hayes, James Garfield, Benjamin Harrison, William McKinley, William Taft, and Warren Harding dominated the White House from 1869 to 1923.

FUNKY FLAG

Ohio is the only state with a flag that is not rectangular. It is a burgee, or "swallowtail" design, which looks like a forked pennant.

PERFECT PITCH

The best pitchers in major league baseball are given the Cy Young Award, named after a brilliant pitcher from Gilmore who retired in 1911 after winning 511 games!

SCARY SCHOOL!

Margaret Hamilton, also known as the Wicked Witch of the West in *The Wizard of Oz*, ran a Cleveland nursery school before becoming an actress. Hopefully she was nicer as Ms. Hamilton!

DOUBLE TAKE

The Twin Days Festival takes place in Twinsburg, naturally. Every August, nearly 3,000 sets of twins take part in sports events, barbeques, and the "Double Take" Parade.

MAN OF TOMORROW

Created by Jerry Siegel and Joe Shuster of Cleveland, Superman first appeared in the early 1930s. Siegel and Shuster sold the Man of Steel to Detective Comics and he took off faster than a speeding bullet!

OHIO

THE BUCKEYE STATE

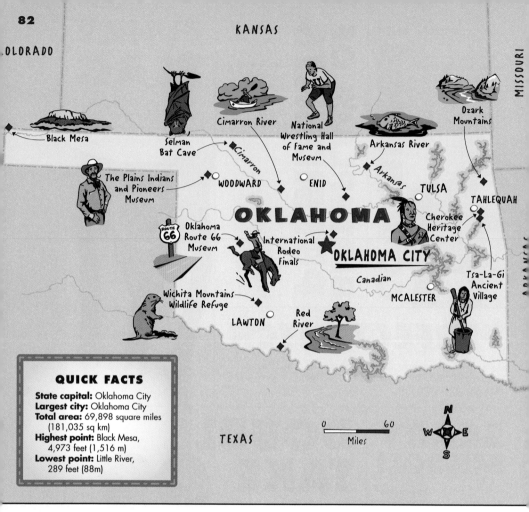

KANSAS

COLORADO

MISSOURI

Black Mesa

Selman
Bat Cave

Cimarron River

Cimarron

WOODWARD

The Plains Indians
and Pioneers
Museum

ROUTE 66

Oklahoma
Route 66
Museum

National
Wrestling Hall
of Fame and
Museum

ENID

International
Rodeo
Finals

Arkansas River

Arkansas

TULSA

Ozark
Mountains

TAHLEQUAH

OKLAHOMA

Cherokee
Heritage
Center

OKLAHOMA CITY

Canadian

MCALESTER

Tsa-La-Gi
Ancient
Village

Wichita Mountains
Wildlife Refuge

LAWTON

Red
River

ARKANSAS

QUICK FACTS

State capital: Oklahoma City
Largest city: Oklahoma City
Total area: 69,898 square miles
(181,035 sq km)
Highest point: Black Mesa,
4,973 feet (1,516 m)
Lowest point: Little River,
289 feet (88m)

TEXAS

N
W   E
S

0   60
Miles

SOONER STATE

Where does Oklahoma's nickname, "The Sooner State," come from? In 1889, some white settlers staked their claims to land before, or "sooner," than they were supposed to.

OILY CAPITOL
BUILDING

The state capitol in Oklahoma City produces more than just legislation—it also produces oil! The building sits atop the active oil wells of the Oklahoma City Oil Field.

GREAT SEAL OF THE STATE OF OKLAHOMA

1907

THOR RELOCATES

Marvel Comics hero Thor has left the Big Apple for Oklahoma! The new writer of the series decided to set Thor's stories near the ancient Heavener Runestone, in Heavener.

PARKING PAIN

When you put a quarter in a parking meter, thank Carl C. Magee of Oklahoma City. He invented the device in 1935, much to the chagrin of drivers everywhere!

COW CHIP CHAMPS

Each spring, the panhandle city of Beaver holds the World Championship Cow Chip Throw! The town's mascot is King Cow Chip, a mound of cow poop wearing a crown.

INDIAN NATION

Oklahoma is home to more American Indian tribes than any other state. In fact, the word "Oklahoma" comes from two Choctaw words that translate as "red people."

WATER POWER

The Pensacola Dam in Grand Lake is the largest multiple arch dam in the world. The 5,145-foot dam has 51 arches and provides power for 24 counties in Oklahoma.

PITT STOP

Brad Pitt, the actor known for his roles in *Thelma & Louise*, *Interview with the Vampire*, and *Babel*, was born William Bradley Pitt in Shawnee in 1963.

Who bombed Boise City during World War II? Oops! The U.S. military accidentally dropped six practice bombs full of sand on the town in 1943. No one was hurt.

BOMB BLUNDER

Sylvan Goldman of Oklahoma City invented the shopping cart in 1937. Everyone rejected the carts until he paid young people in good shape to use them. Then they took off!

CART CRAZE

OKLAHOMA

THE SOONER STATE

WASHINGTON

Lewis and Clark Campsite

Columbia River Maritime Museum

World Forestry Center

Mount Hood Railroad

ASTORIA

PORTLAND

Columbia

PACIFIC OCEAN

QUICK FACTS
State capital: Salem
Largest city: Portland
Total area: 98,381 square miles (254,807 sq km)
Highest point: Mount Hood, 11,239 feet (3,426 m)
Lowest point: Sea level along the Pacific Ocean

Tamastslikt Cultural Institute

John Day Fossil Beds National Monument

Coast Range

Willamette

SALEM

Mission Mill Museum

Cascade Mountains

Deschutes

John Day

Snake

IDAHO

Yaquina Head Lighthouse

OREGON

ONTARIO

National Historic Oregon Trail Interpretive Center

EUGENE

BEND

Newberry National Volcanic Monument

Museum of Natural and Cultural History

COOS BAY

Oregon Dunes National Recreation Area

Crater Lake

Oregon Shakespeare Festival

Great Basin

N W E S

0   50
Miles

Rogue

MEDFORD

Klamath

KLAMATH FALLS

Oregon Caves National Monument

CALIFORNIA

NEVADA

MARBLE CONSISTENCY

The caves at the Oregon Caves National Monument in the Siskiyou Mountains were discovered in 1874. They are natural marble, which keeps the temperature at 44°F year round.

PACHYDERM PROOF

The John Day Fossil Beds in Kimberly are home to some of the world's oldest fossils of the early rhinoceros, an animal that resembled a horse more than today's rhinoceros.

SHORT COMPETITION

The 120-foot D River in Lincoln used to compete with Montana's Roe River to be the "shortest river in the world," a distinction *Guinness World Records* no longer recognizes.

BEING BORING

There is a town in Oregon called Boring. Visitors entering the town are greeted by a sign that says, "Entering Boring." And what's their motto? "Boring—the most exciting place to live!"

STRANGE STANDARD

Unlike any other state flag, the Oregon state flag is double-sided! The front sports the state seal, and the back pictures the state animal, the beaver.

FABULOUS FLOP

Portland-born track star Dick Fosbury won Olympic gold in 1968 by going over the high jump head first and backwards. This now-common method is called the "Fosbury flop"!

MARKETING MAKEOVER

Oregon grows 99% of the entire U.S. commercial crop of filberts. Don't know what a filbert is? You do, actually—"filbert" is just a less glamorous term for "hazelnut"!

DEEP WATERS

Crater Lake National Park is home to the deepest lake in the United States. Crater Lake is more than 1,900 feet deep, and was created when a volcano erupted and collapsed 7,700 years ago!

A TOSS-UP

The name of Oregon's capital in 1851—Portland—was decided in a coin toss when the city founders both wanted to name the city after their hometowns (Boston, Massachusetts, and Portland, Maine).

The world's oldest sandals were found in 1938 by a University of Oregon archaeologist in a cave at Fort Rock. The 10,000-year-old shoes are made of sagebrush bark.

ANCIENT FLIP-FLOPS

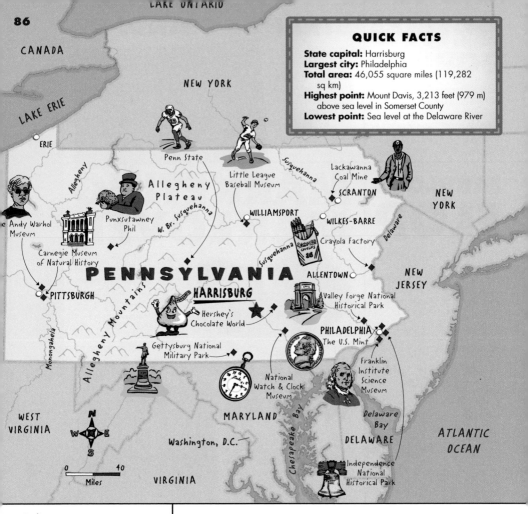

LAKE ONTARIO

CANADA

LAKE ERIE

NEW YORK

ERIE

QUICK FACTS

State capital: Harrisburg
Largest city: Philadelphia
Total area: 46,055 square miles (119,282 sq km)
Highest point: Mount Davis, 3,213 feet (979 m) above sea level in Somerset County
Lowest point: Sea level at the Delaware River

Penn State

Allegheny

Allegheny Plateau

Punxsutawney Phil

W. Br. Susquehanna

Little League Baseball Museum

Susquehanna

Lackawanna Coal Mine

SCRANTON

NEW YORK

Andy Warhol Museum

Carnegie Museum of Natural History

WILLIAMSPORT

WILKES-BARRE

Delaware

Crayola Factory

PENNSYLVANIA

Susquehanna

PITTSBURGH

Allegheny Mountains

Monongahela

HARRISBURG

Hershey's Chocolate World

Gettysburg National Military Park

National Watch & Clock Museum

ALLENTOWN

Valley Forge National Historical Park

PHILADELPHIA
The U.S. Mint

NEW JERSEY

Franklin Institute Science Museum

Delaware Bay

DELAWARE

Chesapeake Bay

ATLANTIC OCEAN

WEST VIRGINIA

N W E S

0   40
Miles

MARYLAND

Washington, D.C.

VIRGINIA

Independence National Historical Park

Punxsutawney is home to Phil, the legendary groundhog who leaves his burrow on February 2 and "predicts" how much longer winter will last. He made his first observance in 1886.

WHERE'S THE "H"?

In 1890, the United States Postal Office dropped the "h" in "Pittsburgh." Concerned citizens mounted an effort to get their "h" back and it was officially restored in 1911.

MEETING THE ENEMY

Commodore Oliver Hazard Perry defeated the British on Lake Erie during the War of 1812, reporting his victory with the words, "We have met the enemy and they are ours!"

PHILLY LOVES PRETZELS

The average Philadelphian eats over 20 pounds of soft pretzels per year! (To give you an idea of how much Philly loves pretzels, the average American eats two pounds per year.)

SHORT SPEECH

President Abraham Lincoln's famous Gettysburg Address in Gettysburg is one of the most quoted political speeches in history—and also one of the shortest. It was just over two minutes long.

FLEXIBLE ARTIST

The artist N.C. Wyeth of Chadds Ford illustrated the children's classic *Treasure Island* as well as ads for Cream of Wheat and Coca-Cola. (Artists have to eat, too, you know!)

MONUMENT TO BEN

In Philadelphia, a 101-foot-tall, 60-ton sculpture of a lightning strike, a kite, and a key commemorates Ben Franklin's experiment that forever changed our understanding of electricity.

YUMMY COLORS

Take a tour of the Crayola Crayon factory in Easton and learn how wax and pigment combine to make colors like macaroni and cheese, mango tango, and jazzberry jam.

DRINK Coca-Cola
IT'S THE REFRESHING THING TO DO

Jim Thorpe of Carlisle, arguably the greatest athlete of the 20th century, played professional baseball, won two events at the 1912 Olympics, and was a high school football star.

AMAZING ATHLETE

MILLIONS OF KISSES

Factories in Hershey, also known as the "Sweetest Place on Earth," produce 80 million chocolate Kisses a day. How many do you think you could eat in one sitting?

ATLANTIC OCEAN

QUICK FACTS

Capital: San Juan
Largest city: San Juan
Total area: 5,325 square miles (13,792 sq km)
Highest point: Cerro de Punta, 4,390 feet (1,338 m)
Lowest point: Sea level along the Atlantic Ocean

Arecibo Observatory

Arecibo Lighthouse and Historical Park

San Cristóbal Fort

SAN JUAN

El Yunque National Forest

ARECIBO

BAYAMÓN

Culebra Island

Caguana Indian Ceremonial Park

Arecibo

Manati

La Plata

Loíza

CAROLINA

Añasco

PUERTO RICO

Vieques Passage

Vieques Sound

MAYAGÜEZ

Tres Picachos

Cordillera Central

CAGUAS

Vieques Island

Mona Passage

PONCE

Las Cabezas de San Juan State Park

Cartagena Lagoon Natural Reserve

Caja de Muertos

Cabo Rojo Lighthouse

Ponce Museum of Art

Parque de Las Ciencias Luis A. Ferré

CARIBBEAN SEA

0   20
Miles

WHO WAS FIRST?

Long before the Spanish or the Americans showed up, Puerto Rico belonged to the Taíno Indians, and was called Borinquen, which means the "Land of the Mighty Lord."

VOTING RESTRICTIONS

Puerto Ricans have been U.S. citizens since 1917. However, they can vote in presidential elections only if they reside in one of the 50 states.

VOTE

CLOSE QUARTERS

Puerto Rico is one of the most densely populated islands on the planet. With a population of close to 4 million, there are 1,000 people per square mile!

BIT OF BACKGROUND

The island of Puerto Rico was ceded to the U.S. by Spain in 1898, after the Spanish-American War. In 1952, Puerto Rico became a self-governing territory of the U.S.

AWARDS APLENTY

Rita Moreno of Humacao was the only Hispanic woman to win an Emmy, a Tony, an Oscar, and a Grammy. This great talent was on Broadway by the time she was 13!

TOP TELESCOPE

The Arecibo Observatory, near Arecibo, has the biggest radio telescope in the world. Scientists and students from all over use the telescope for planetary—and extraterrestrial—research.

THE OLD CITY

San Juan, Puerto Rico's capital, has some of the first forts ever built by the Spanish in the Americas, and the oldest parts of the city still have original cobblestone streets.

TREE WONDERLAND

El Yunque National Forest is the only tropical forest in the national forest system. It has 240 species of trees, 23 of which are only found in El Yunque!

There are nearly a million Puerto Ricans in New York, many of whom consider themselves Nuyorican, a name that combines "Puerto Rican" and "New York."

NUYORICAN PRIDE

HEART OF GOLD

Baseball legend Roberto Clemente of Barrio San Antón played for the Brooklyn Dodgers and Pittsburgh Pirates before dying in a 1972 plane crash while bringing aid to Nicaraguan earthquake victims.

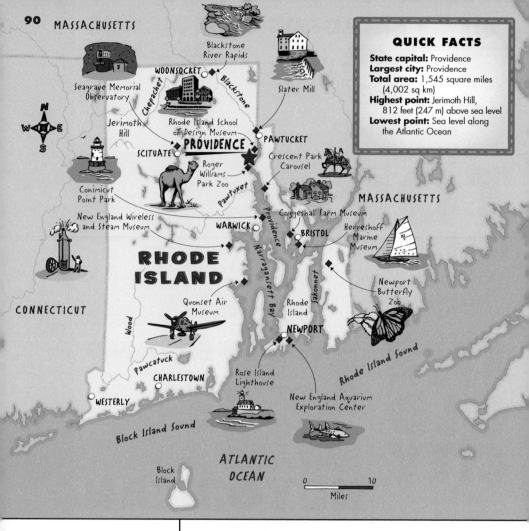

Blackstone
River Rapids

WOONSOCKET

Blackstone

Slater Mill

Seagrave Memorial
Observatory

Chepachet

Jerimoth
Hill

Rhode Island School
of Design Museum
PROVIDENCE

PAWTUCKET

SCITUATE

Roger
Williams
Park Zoo

Crescent Park
Carousel

Conimicut
Point Park

Pawtuxet

MASSACHUSETTS

New England Wireless
and Steam Museum

Providence

WARWICK

Coggeshall Farm Museum

BRISTOL

Herreshoff
Marine
Museum

RHODE
ISLAND

Narragansett Bay

Quonset Air
Museum

Rhode
Island

Newport
Butterfly
Zoo

Sakonnet

CONNECTICUT

Wood

NEWPORT

Pawcatuck

CHARLESTOWN

Rose Island
Lighthouse

Rhode Island Sound

WESTERLY

New England Aquarium
Exploration Center

Block Island Sound

Block
Island

ATLANTIC
OCEAN

0   10
Miles

QUICK FACTS

State capital: Providence
Largest city: Providence
Total area: 1,545 square miles
(4,002 sq km)
Highest point: Jerimoth Hill,
812 feet (247 m) above sea level
Lowest point: Sea level along
the Atlantic Ocean

ROLL ON!

In the summer of 1866,
a roller-skating club
built the country's first
public skating rink in
a Newport hotel, and
vacationers
went crazy
over the latest
fad on wheels!

SMALLEST STATE?

Though it is the smallest
state in the nation,
Rhode Island consists
of 36 islands as well as
mainland, and has over
400 miles of coastline.

RIVER MIGHT

In 1789 on the Blackstone River in Pawtucket, Samuel Slater, aka the
"Father of the American Industrial Revolution," designed and built the
first American textile mill powered by water.

WELL-DRESSED TERMITE

Nibbles Woodaway is a 58-foot-long hurricane-proof blue termite who lives on top of New England Pest Control in Providence—and who dresses appropriately for the holidays!

TEMPLE IN DISGUISE

In 1776 in Newport, the British used Touro Synagogue—the oldest temple in America—as a hospital, in order to ensure its survival during the Revolutionary War.

RHODE WHAT?!

Rhode Island isn't officially called Rhode Island. The state's full name is "The State of Rhode Island and Providence Plantations." (The latter refers to the mainland part of the state.)

FAMOUS FOURTH FEST

Bristol is home to one of the oldest 4th of July parades in the nation, first held in 1785. A red, white, and blue stripe on the town's main street marks the parade route year round.

FACIAL HAIR FAME

Ambrose Burnside, the Civil War general who commanded Fort Adams in Newport, was famous for his facial hair. Barbers called his odd bristles "burnsides," and later, "sideburns."

MOVE OVER, PONY

America's first auto race on a track took place at the Narragansett Trotting Park in Cranston, in 1896. Just imagine how confused the horses must have been!

"UNDERDOG IS HERE!"

Providence is proud to call Underdog its own. The 2007 movie, *Underdog*, about a dog with super powers (and a fancy cape) was shot in over a dozen locations around town.

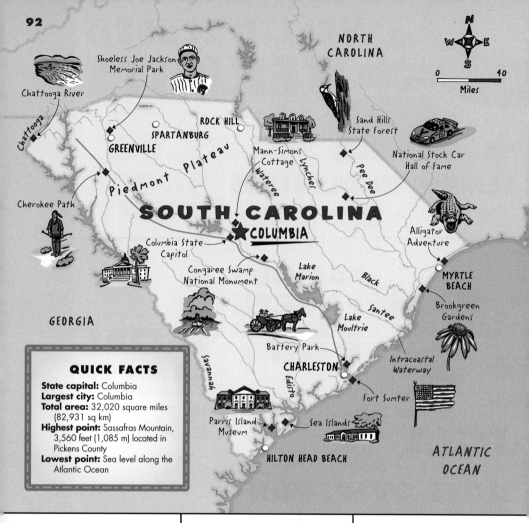

NORTH CAROLINA

Chattooga River

Shoeless Joe Jackson Memorial Park

Chattooga

ROCK HILL
SPARTANBURG
GREENVILLE

Sand Hills State Forest

Mann-Simons Cottage

Wateree

Lynches

Pee Dee

National Stock Car Hall of Fame

Piedmont Plateau

Cherokee Path

SOUTH CAROLINA
★**COLUMBIA**

Alligator Adventure

Columbia State Capitol

Congaree Swamp National Monument

Lake Marion

Black

Santee

Lake Moultrie

MYRTLE BEACH

Brookgreen Gardens

GEORGIA

Savannah

Battery Park

CHARLESTON

Intracoastal Waterway

Edisto

Fort Sumter

Parris Island Museum

Sea Islands

HILTON HEAD BEACH

ATLANTIC OCEAN

N W E S
0   40
Miles

QUICK FACTS

State capital: Columbia
Largest city: Columbia
Total area: 32,020 square miles (82,931 sq km)
Highest point: Sassafras Mountain, 3,560 feet (1,085 m) located in Pickens County
Lowest point: Sea level along the Atlantic Ocean

SOUTHERN PEACH CAPITOL

The one-million-gallon Peachoid Water Tower in Gaffney attempts to set the record straight about exactly who produces the most peaches in the South. (It's South Carolina, not Georgia.)

GAFFNEY GAFFNEY

WHAT'S RETIREMENT?

U.S. Senator Strom Thurmond of Edgefield left office in 2003, when he was 100 years old, making him the longest-serving senator in U.S. history.

THAT CHARLESTON STYLE

The Charleston, the dance craze of the 1920s popularized by flappers, was believed to have been created around 1900 by African Americans living off the coast of—you guessed it—Charleston.

THE FIRST SHOT

The Civil War began on April 12, 1861, at Fort Sumter in Charleston Harbor. Confederate forces fired the first shot and won the fort, holding on to it for four years.

PUTT-PUTT CHAMPS

Myrtle Beach has the most miniature golf courses in the United States (over 40). Not surprisingly, it also hosts the Masters National Pro Mini Golf Championship!

FIELD OF HISTORY

Spartanburg is home to the country's oldest minor league baseball stadium, Duncan Park, which hosted its first game in 1926. Locals are currently trying to save the park from disrepair.

ONE GIANT STEP

In 1999, Nancy Ruth Mace of Goose Creek became the first woman to graduate from The Citadel, one of the country's premier military colleges, ending 150 years of single-gender education there.

SAVE THE FLYTRAP!

The Venus Flytrap, a carnivorous plant native to South Carolina that actually catches its prey and digests it, is disappearing, owing to land development and encroaching humans.

Frogmore Stew, named after a fishing town near Beaufort, is a one-pot, boiled meal of shrimp, crab, and corn, traditionally served on newspaper! (There are no frogs involved.)

LOWCOUNTRY BOIL!

James Brown, the Barnwell-born singer who was inducted into the Rock and Roll Hall of Fame in 1986, was called the "Godfather of Soul" and "Soul Brother Number One."

"I FEEL GOOD!"

SOUTH CAROLINA
THE PALMETTO STATE

NORTH DAKOTA

Fort Sisseton State Historical Park

MINNESOTA

Grand

Moreau

Missouri

ABERDEEN

Motorcycle Museum & Hall of Fame

South Dakota Air and Space Museum

Great Lake Plains
Oahe

WATERTOWN

South Dakota Art Museum

SOUTH DAKOTA

Cheyenne

Big Sioux

Black Hills National Forest

Mount Rushmore

PIERRE

South Dakota State Capitol

James

RAPID CITY

White

CHAMBERLAIN

Great Plains Zoo

SIOUX FALLS

Custer State Park

Badlands National Park

Akta Lakota Museum & Cultural Center

Missouri

Jewel Cave National Monument

Sitting Bull and Sacagawea Monuments

South Dakota Hall of Fame

YANKTON

IOWA

NEBRASKA

USS South Dakota Battleship Memorial

QUICK FACTS

State capital: Pierre
Largest city: Sioux Falls
Total area: 77,117 square miles (199,731 sq km)
Highest point: Harney Peak, 7,242 feet (2,207 m), in Pennington County
Lowest point: Big Stone Lake, 966 feet (294 m), in Roberts County

N W E S

0   40
Miles

FAMOUS FACE

Tom Brokaw grew up in Yankton, graduated from the University of South Dakota, and went on to become one of our nation's most famous network news anchors.

MOTORCYCLE MADNESS

Every August, the population of Spearfish explodes when motorcyclists from all over the country arrive for the Sturgis Rally, started in 1938, which features races and road tours.

DANCES WITH OSCAR

The movie *Dances With Wolves*, which won seven Oscars in 1990 and tells the story of a U.S. lieutenant who befriends Sioux Indians, was filmed primarily in the Black Hills.

The Flaming Fountain in Pierre is exactly what it sounds like—a fountain on fire! It's fed by natural gas and looks beautiful, but smells bad!

FIERY FOUNTAIN

ACCURATE TRANSLATION

Badlands National Park derived its name from the Lakota Indians, who called the area *mako sica*, meaning, "land bad." Its desolate beauty pretty much speaks for itself.

SIZEABLE SCULPTURE

When it is finished, the 563-foot-tall Black Hills monument to Crazy Horse—the Indian leader who fought at the Battle of Little Big Horn—will surpass Mount Rushmore as the largest sculpture in the world.

PRESIDENTIAL CRANIUMS

President's Park, in Lead, features giant, 16- to 20-foot-tall busts of all the U.S. presidents arranged in chronological order. (George Washington—Mr. Number One—gets a view of the snack bar.)

PIONEER GIRL

In *Little Town on the Prairie*, part of her Little House series, Laura Ingalls Wilder wrote about pioneer life in DeSmet.

LAWLESS LAWMAN

Wild Bill Hickok, a lawman with a criminal record, was killed in 1876 in Deadwood when he broke his own rule and played poker in a chair that didn't face the door.

CORN ART

Mitchell is home to the famous Corn Palace, which dates to 1892. The palace is redecorated each year with new murals of life in South Dakota—made out of corn!

MITCHELL CORN PALACE

SOUTH DAKOTA

THE MOUNT RUSHMORE STATE

ILLINOIS

INDIANA

OHIO

WEST VIRGINIA

KENTUCKY

MISSOURI

World's Largest Guitar

Bristol Motor Speedway

VIRGINIA

Tennessee National Wildlife Refuge

Country Music Hall of Fame and Museum

Knoxville Zoo

NASHVILLE Cumberland

Tennessee State Capitol

Musicians Hall of Fame and Museum

KNOXVILLE

NORTH CAROLINA

TENNESSEE

Cumberland Caverns

Great Smoky Mountains National Park

MEMPHIS

Sharpe Planetarium

CHATTANOOGA

NASCAR SpeedPark

SOUTH CAROLINA

Elvis Presley's Graceland

Creative Discovery Museum

GEORGIA

MISSISSIPPI

ALABAMA

N W E S

0   50
Miles

QUICK FACTS

State capital: Nashville
Largest city: Memphis
Total area: 42,143 square miles (109,151 sq km)
Highest point: Clingmans Dome, 6,643 feet (2,025 m), located in Sevier County
Lowest point: Mississippi River in Shelby County, 178 feet (54 m)

THE KING'S HOUSE

Graceland, the Memphis home of Elvis Presley, is visited by about 600,000 people a year. The only home with more visitors per year is the White House!

"BE A GOOD BOY!"

A woman's right to vote hinged on one man in 1920: Tennessee representative Harry Burn. He planned to vote against suffrage, but a note from his mother changed his mind.

STRIKE THREE

In 1931, 17-year-old Jackie Mitchell of the Chattanooga Lookouts struck out Babe Ruth and Lou Gehrig during an exhibition game against the Yankees. *She* was fired a few days later.

THE VOLUNTEER STATE

Tennessee earned its nickname during the War of 1812, when volunteer soldiers from Tennessee served valiantly under General Andrew Jackson at the Battle of New Orleans.

A PIECE OF GREECE

Greece in Nashville? Yup! A full-scale homage to the Parthenon in Athens was built for Tennessee's 1897 Centennial Exposition as a monument to classic architecture.

INTERESTING CHOICE

Even though the country-gospel group the Oak Ridge Boys was based in Knoxville, they took their name from nearby Oak Ridge, where the atomic bomb was being developed.

PARADING DUCKS

The Peabody Memphis hotel features the Duck March, during which ducks parade through the lobby to the Peabody fountain daily. (Duck is not on the menu at the hotel.)

SHORT BUT SWEET

The Bristol Motor Speedway is only half a mile long—but it's known as the World's Fastest Half Mile. Racing on it has been compared to "flying fighter jets in a gymnasium."

WHAT A VIEW!

On a clear day, Tennesseans say you can see seven states from the top of Chattanooga's Lookout Mountain: Tennessee, Georgia, Kentucky, Virginia, North Carolina, South Carolina, and Alabama.

COUNTRY MUSIC GOLDMINE

The Grand Ole Opry, the nation's longest-running live radio broadcast, has been on the air since 1925.

QUICK FACTS

State capital: Austin
Largest city: Houston
Total area: 268,581 square
 miles (695,625 sq km)
Highest point: Guadalupe Peak,
 8,749 feet (2,667 m)
Lowest point: Sea level along
 the Gulf of Mexico

PROPER CHILI

Texans are fond of saying, "If you know beans about chili, you know chili ain't got no beans." Texans put beef and tomatoes in their chili, and leave the beans for burritos.

INFURIATING ARTIST?

Robert Rauschenberg, born in Port Arthur in 1925, was famous for paintings called "Singular Forms," featuring one solid color on a canvas. The paintings continue to infuriate—and enrapture—today.

AVIATRICES, UNITE!

Avenger Field in Sweetwater was an airbase for female pilots in World War II. From 1943 to 1944, the base contained the only military flight school for women in the world.

SO MANY COWS!

Texas has 14 million cattle. To give you an idea of exactly what that means, 46 states have fewer people than Texas has cattle. (How many cow chips do they have?!)

FROM BIG TO BOLD

When Alaska became a state in 1959, Texas had to change "largest" to "boldest" in its state song. (Texas is over 268,000 square miles; Alaska is over 663,000 square miles.)

Space Center Houston, the visitors' center at NASA's Johnson Space Center, is home to the Blast Off Theater, which allows visitors to experience a simulated space launch—complete with billowing smoke!

BLAST OFF!

INSPIRED BY A KINGDOM

Think the buildings at the University of Texas at El Paso look like the mountain kingdom of Bhutan? You're right! The university's architecture is modeled after Bhutanese monasteries.

GRAND OLD FLAG(S)

The flags of France, Spain, Mexico, the Republic of Texas, the Confederate States of America, and the United States have all flown over Texas at least once since 1685.

SPELLING OUTLAW

Bonnie Parker was the Dallas citywide spelling bee champion before she fell in love with Clyde Barrow in 1930 and became half of the infamous outlaw duo Bonnie & Clyde.

HORRIBLE HURRICANE

The Galveston hurricane of 1900 was the deadliest natural disaster in U.S. history. Over 5,000 people died in the raging storm and almost the entire city was destroyed.

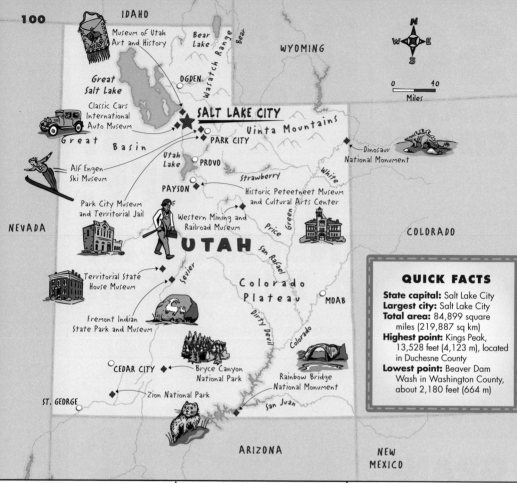

IDAHO

Museum of Utah
Art and History

Bear
Lake

WYOMING

Bear

Wasatch Range

Great
Salt Lake

OGDEN

SALT LAKE CITY

Classic Cars
International
Auto Museum

Uinta Mountains

Great   Basin

PARK CITY

Alf Engen
Ski Museum

Utah
Lake

PROVO

Dinosaur
National Monument

White

Strawberry

NEVADA

PAYSON

Historic Peteetneet Museum
and Cultural Arts Center

Park City Museum
and Territorial Jail

Western Mining and
Railroad Museum

Green

UTAH

Price

COLORADO

Territorial State
House Museum

Sevier

San Rafael

Colorado
Plateau

MOAB

Fremont Indian
State Park and Museum

Dirty Devil

Colorado

CEDAR CITY

Bryce Canyon
National Park

Rainbow Bridge
National Monument

ST. GEORGE

Zion National Park

San Juan

ARIZONA

NEW
MEXICO

N
W   E
S

0   40
Miles

QUICK FACTS

State capital: Salt Lake City
Largest city: Salt Lake City
Total area: 84,899 square
miles (219,887 sq km)
Highest point: Kings Peak,
13,528 feet (4,123 m), located
in Duchesne County
Lowest point: Beaver Dam
Wash in Washington County,
about 2,180 feet (664 m)

AN
OUTLAW
IS BORN

Robert Leroy Parker, born in 1866 in
Beaver, changed his name to Butch
Cassidy after he worked as a butcher.
He chose "Cassidy" to honor his
criminal mentor, Mike Cassidy.

SPEEDING
ON
SALT

Speed racers of all kinds travel to the
Bonneville Salt Flats, one of the
flattest places on earth, to race.
Hundreds of land speed
records have been
set—and broken—
there!

LA LA
LAAAAA!

The world-famous and Grammy Award-
winning Mormon Tabernacle Choir,
based in Salt Lake City, was founded in
1847. The 360-member choir has sung
at five presidential inaugurations.

STONE RAINBOW

Lake Powell is home to Rainbow Bridge, a 290-foot-high natural stone arch formed over a creek. The Navajo call the arch "Nonnezoshe," which means "rainbow turned to stone."

BELLYBUTTON TOWN

Levan is in the center of Utah. Since "Levan" spells "navel" backward, some suspect that whoever named the town had a good sense of humor. (Or a knack for coincidences.)

GREEN JELL-O SALAD

If you're a fan of Jell-O, Utah is the place for you. Green Jell-O salad is a staple in Utah, some versions of which include pineapple, cream cheese, and Sprite. (Gulp.)

DINO LOVER'S DELIGHT

Dinosaur National Monument near Vernal is home to the Dinosaur Quarry, a steep wall of rock that contains over 1,500 dinosaur bones, some of which are still in skeleton form.

RAILROAD'S GOLDEN MOMENT

In May of 1869 at Promontory Summit, a golden spike was used to symbolically join the Union Pacific and Central Pacific lines, forming America's first trans-continental railroad.

119

Vernal
UTAH'S DINOSAUR LAND

DIGGING IN

According to NASA, the Bingham Canyon Open Pit Copper Mine in Salt Lake Valley is one of the largest holes ever dug by humans. It is almost a mile deep and 2.5 miles wide.

THELMA & LOUISE

Dead Horse Point National Park doubles as the Grand Canyon in the final scene of the 1991 Oscar-winning film *Thelma & Louise* when the women drive their convertible off a cliff.

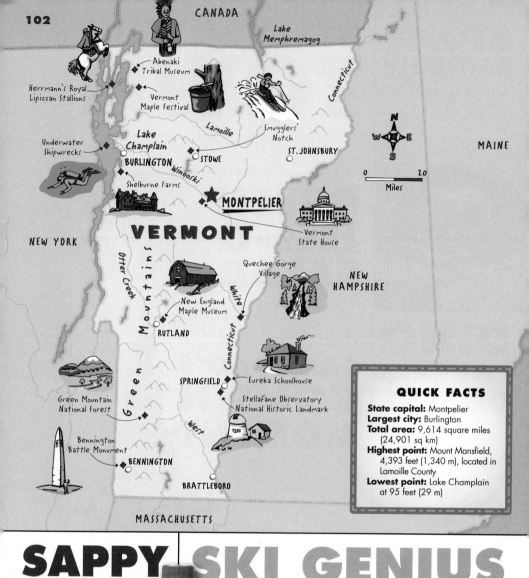

CANADA

Lake Memphremagog

Herrmann's Royal Lipizzan Stallions

Abenaki Tribal Museum

Vermont Maple Festival

Smugglers' Notch

Lamoille

Connecticut

MAINE

Underwater Shipwrecks

Lake Champlain

BURLINGTON ◆ STOWE

Winooski

ST. JOHNSBURY

N W E S

0   20
Miles

Shelburne Farms

★ MONTPELIER

VERMONT

Vermont State House

NEW YORK

Otter Creek

Green Mountains

Quechee Gorge Village

White

NEW HAMPSHIRE

New England Maple Museum

RUTLAND

Connecticut

Green Mountain National Forest

SPRINGFIELD

Eureka Schoolhouse

Stellafane Observatory National Historic Landmark

West

Bennington Battle Monument

BENNINGTON

BRATTLEBORO

MASSACHUSETTS

QUICK FACTS

State capital: Montpelier
Largest city: Burlington
Total area: 9,614 square miles (24,901 sq km)
Highest point: Mount Mansfield, 4,393 feet (1,340 m), located in Lamoille County
Lowest point: Lake Champlain at 95 feet (29 m)

SAPPY STATE

It takes 40 gallons of sap to make one gallon of maple syrup, and Vermont is the largest producer of maple syrup in the U.S. So it's fair to call the state "sappy."

SKI GENIUS

Bunny Bertram of Woodstock developed the first motorized rope-tow ski lift in 1934. His stroke of genius? To power the lift using a Model T Ford engine.

ROAD TRIP!

In 1903, Dr. Horatio Nelson Jackson of Burlington became the first person to drive a car across the country. He traveled with Bud, his goggle-wearing bulldog, in a car named *Vermont*.

WHAT A HEADACHE

A plaque for Phineas Gage can be found in Cavendish. The railroad blaster suffered a metal rod driven through his skull in 1848. Not only did he survive, he never lost consciousness!

THE SNOWFLAKE MAN

Photographer Wilson A. Bentley became known as "the snowflake man" when he photographed a single snowflake in 1885. He went on to photograph 5,000, proving that no two snowflakes are alike!

AHEAD OF THE CURVE

Vermont was the first place in the nation to outlaw slavery. It was written into the original Constitution in 1777, before statehood, when Vermont was known as the Vermont Republic.

ESCAPE TO VERMONT

The Von Trapp family, featured in the musical and film *The Sound of Music*, settled in Stowe and opened the Trapp Family Lodge after escaping Austria during World War II.

ICE CREAM PIGS

Reportedly unused ice cream from the Ben & Jerry's factory in Waterbury goes to local pigs—except for one now-retired flavor. They turned up their noses at Mint Oreo Cookie.

MONSTROUS COUSINS

The Loch Ness Monster has a "cousin" who lives in Lake Champlain. Locals have named the beast Champ, who was first sighted in 1609 by explorer Samuel de Champlain.

WHALE OF A TALE

In 1849, some very puzzled railroad workers found a whale fossil in Charlotte. What was a whale doing in Vermont? During the ice age, Vermont was basically underwater.

VERMONT

THE GREEN MOUNTAIN STATE

QUICK FACTS

State capital: Richmond
Largest city: Virginia Beach
Total area: 42,774 square miles
(110,784 sq km)
Highest point: Mount Rogers at
5,722 feet (1,744 m)
Lowest point: Sea level along
the Atlantic Ocean

SONGBIRD SMITH

Singer Kate Smith, whose famous recording of "God Bless America" is often heard at Yankee Stadium during the 7th inning stretch, was born in Greenville in 1907.

WORLD'S BIGGEST OFFICE

Arlington is home to the world's largest office building: the Pentagon, also known as the Department of Defense. It has 3.7 million square feet of space, and over 23,000 employees!

ESPIONAGE QUEEN

Elizabeth "Crazy Bet" Van Lew of Richmond ran a 12-person spy ring for the Union during the Civil War. The great spy is in the Military Intelligence Hall of Fame.

ROCK MUSIC

The Luray Caverns in Luray are a series of caves full of stalactites and stalagmites, including the Great Stalacpipe Organ, a musical instrument formed out of stalactites in the cave.

BACKWARD BOJANGLES

Richmond's Bill "Bojangles" Robinson, a famous tap dancer and film star, set a world record for running backward, completing a 75-yard backward dash in 8.2 seconds.

A BUSY WOMAN!

Lucy Diggs Slowe of Berryville established the first junior high school in Washington, D.C., and in 1917 became the first African American woman to win the American Tennis Association tournament.

GORY WARNING

Virginia authorities, tired of thieving pirates, hung Blackbeard's skull at the meeting point of the Hampton and James rivers, which is now known as Blackbeard Point.

GOD OF THE SEA

Virginia Beach welcomes its visitors with a 34-foot-tall statue of Neptune, the Roman god of the sea. He is accompanied by two dolphins, a loggerhead turtle, and an octopus.

ODD COINCIDENCE

Thomas Jefferson, author of the Declaration of Independence, was born in Shadwell in 1743. The founding father died 83 years later on the 4th of July, the document's 50th anniversary.

LAND OF PEACE

Two wars ended in Virginia. The Revolutionary War ended with the Battle of Yorktown in 1781 and the Civil War ended at the Appomattox Court House in 1865.

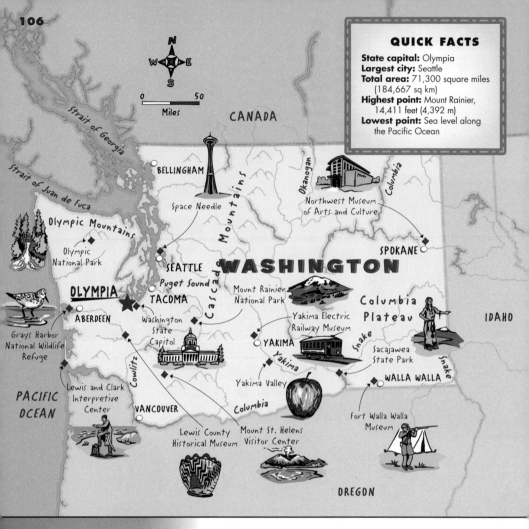

CANADA

Strait of Georgia

Strait of Juan de Fuca

Olympic Mountains

Olympic National Park

PACIFIC OCEAN

Grays Harbor National Wildlife Refuge

BELLINGHAM

Space Needle

SEATTLE

Puget Sound

OLYMPIA

TACOMA

ABERDEEN

Washington State Capitol

Lewis and Clark Interpretive Center

VANCOUVER

Cascade Mountains

WASHINGTON

Mount Rainier National Park

Cowlitz

Lewis County Historical Museum

Mount St. Helens Visitor Center

Okanogan

Columbia

Northwest Museum of Arts and Culture

SPOKANE

Columbia Plateau

Yakima Electric Railway Museum

YAKIMA

Yakima

Yakima Valley

Columbia

Snake

Sacajawea State Park

WALLA WALLA

Snake

Fort Walla Walla Museum

IDAHO

OREGON

EARTHQUAKES AND VOLCANOES

In 1980, an earthquake caused the north face of the active volcano Mount St. Helens to collapse. Dust and ash spewed into the sky and blocked out the sun for days.

GEORGE, WASHINGTON

There is a town in Washington named George. This of course means that the last line of envelopes addressed to the city's residents says, "George, Washington"!

WEIRD GEOGRAPHY

If you're planning to travel to Point Roberts from any place in the U.S., bring your passport. In order to get to the U.S. town by car, you must pass through Canada!

GOOEY DUCKS

Geoducks, pronounced "gooey ducks," are giant clams that can weigh up to 10 pounds, sporting 9-inch shells. These monstrous "ducks" can be found on Washington's Pacific coast.

ELECTRIFYING RIVER

The Grand Coulee Dam on the Columbia River is the greatest source of electricity in the United States. It provides one third of America's hydroelectric power!

JAVA JIVE

A 25-foot-high coffee pot built in Tacoma in 1927 is not only still standing, but it has been home to Bob's Java Jive—a coffee shop, bar, and music venue—since 1955.

In Everett, it is illegal for a hypnotist to display a hypnotized person in a store window for advertising purposes. The penalty is a $500 fine and up to six months in jail!

HYPNOTISTS, BEWARE!

GALLOPING GERTIE

The Tacoma Narrows Bridge, which was over a mile long and 39 feet wide, swayed so violently that locals called it "Galloping Gertie." It collapsed four months after opening in 1940.

WORLD'S OLDEST CELEBRITY

The Kennewick Man is a 9,300-year-old skeleton that was discovered by visitors watching hydroplane races in 1996 along the Columbia River. It's one of the oldest skeletons ever found in the Americas.

STINKY FOREST

At 7,470 acres, the Ginkgo Petrified Forest near Kittitas is possibly the largest of its kind in the world. (Hopefully petrified ginkgo trees aren't nearly as stinky as non-petrified ginkgo trees!)

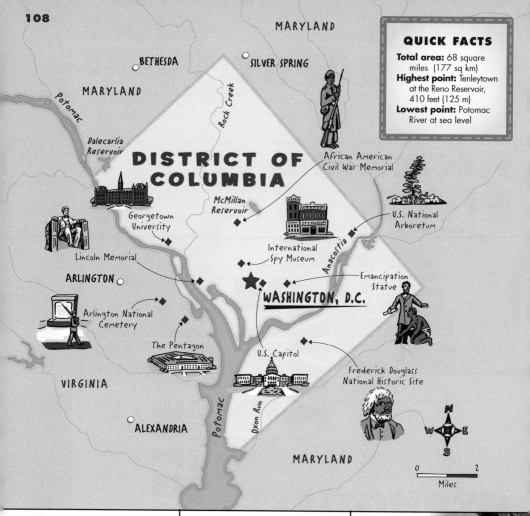

MARYLAND

BETHESDA

SILVER SPRING

MARYLAND

Potomac

Rock Creek

Dalecarlia
Reservoir

DISTRICT OF
COLUMBIA

African American
Civil War Memorial

McMillan
Reservoir

Georgetown
University

International
Spy Museum

U.S. National
Arboretum

Anacostia

Lincoln Memorial

ARLINGTON

Emancipation
Statue

★ WASHINGTON, D.C.

Arlington National
Cemetery

The Pentagon

U.S. Capitol

Frederick Douglass
National Historic Site

VIRGINIA

Dixon Run

ALEXANDRIA

Potomac

MARYLAND

N
W E
S

0   2
Miles

QUICK FACTS

Total area: 68 square
miles (177 sq km)
Highest point: Tenleytown
at the Reno Reservoir,
410 feet (125 m)
Lowest point: Potomac
River at sea level

WORLD TRAVELER

During Eleanor
Roosevelt's first
year as First
Lady, she logged
38,000 miles of
domestic travel.
She was later
given the title
"First Lady of
the World."

BAZILLIONS OF BOOKS!

The Library of Congress is the
world's largest library, with over 120
million items! Every day, 22,000 new
items arrive and 10,000 become
part of the permanent collection.

PANDA-MONIUM!

Some of
America's most
powerful
celebrities live in
D.C., but no one
draws more crowds
on a daily basis
than Tian
Tian and Mei
Xiang, the giant
pandas at the
National Zoo!

E = MC²

The Einstein Memorial on the grounds of the National Academy of Sciences depicts Einstein holding a piece of paper containing three equations summarizing the genius's greatest contributions to science.

WASHINGTON'S CHERRY TREES

In 1912, Japan gave 3,020 cherry trees to Washington. First Lady Helen Taft planted the first tree in a ceremony that inspired what has become Washington's annual Cherry Blossom Festival.

MODEST GEORGE

President George Washington did not like calling the nation's capital "Washington," so he called it the "Federal City" instead. Our first president was very modest!

THE DUKE

Duke Ellington, who began playing piano at age seven, was a brilliant bandleader from D.C. who won countless Grammy Awards and was posthumously recognized by the Pulitzer Prize committee.

COLOSSAL COLUMNS

The National Building Museum has some of the world's largest Corinthian columns (columns with a fluted shape and ornate designs at the top). They are 75 feet tall and 8 feet across.

ROGUE CITY

Washington, D.C., is the only city in the U.S. that is not part of a state. It is regulated by the federal government and officially called the "District of Columbia."

FUN WITH POLITICS!

Appropriately, Stephen Colbert, political satirist and hilarious host of Comedy Central's The Colbert Report, was born in Washington, D.C., in 1964. Must have been something in the water...

THE COLBERT REPORT

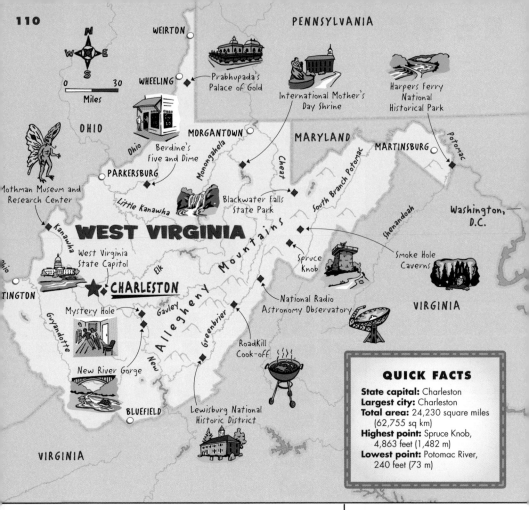

PENNSYLVANIA

WEIRTON

WHEELING

Prabhupada's Palace of Gold

International Mother's Day Shrine

Harpers Ferry National Historical Park

OHIO

MORGANTOWN

MARYLAND

MARTINSBURG

Berdine's Five and Dime

Ohio

Monongahela

Cheat

South Branch Potomac

Potomac

PARKERSBURG

Mothman Museum and Research Center

Little Kanawha

Blackwater Falls State Park

Shenandoah

Washington, D.C.

WEST VIRGINIA

Kanawha

West Virginia State Capitol

Elk

Spruce Knob

Smoke Hole Caverns

VIRGINIA

TINGTON

CHARLESTON

Mystery Hole

Gauley

Allegheny Mountains

National Radio Astronomy Observatory

Guyandotte

New

Greenbrier

New River Gorge

RoadKill Cook-off

BLUEFIELD

Lewisburg National Historic District

VIRGINIA

QUICK FACTS

State capital: Charleston
Largest city: Charleston
Total area: 24,230 square miles (62,755 sq km)
Highest point: Spruce Knob, 4,863 feet (1,482 m)
Lowest point: Potomac River, 240 feet (73 m)

TRAVELING IN STYLE

Students at West Virginia University in Morgantown travel their campus by train! The Personal Rapid Transit, or PRT, carries 15,000 people per day during the school year.

OLD NEW RIVER

The New River is thought to be the oldest river in North America. Unlike most rivers, the New River flows south to north, possibly because it was there before the rest of the landscape!

POWER SHIFT

During the Civil War, the strategically located city of Romney is said to have changed hands between the Union army and the Confederate army a whopping 56 times!

CAPITAL CRAZINESS

In 1863, West Virginia's capital was Wheeling. Then it was officially moved to Charleston, then back to Wheeling. Finally, in 1877, West Virginians voted and they chose Charleston. (Got that?)

WEST VIRGINIA

THE PERFECT LIE

Charleston's Vandalia Gathering has three types of competition each May: one for bakers, one for musicians—and one for liars. Storytellers compete to see who can tell the biggest lie!

THANKS, MR. PRESIDENT

West Virginia is the only state whose statehood was proclaimed by the president. Abraham Lincoln declared West Virginia's statehood in 1863, with the understanding that it would stop practicing slavery.

DOME COMPETITION

The capitol building in Charleston has the tallest dome of all the state capitols. At 293 feet, the dome is 5 feet taller than the capitol dome in Washington, D.C.

LITERACY LAWS

In 1835, three men and one woman in Wheeling were charged with a bizarre crime: teaching African Americans to read. At that time, it was illegal to educate slaves.

FAMOUS FEUD

The Hatfields and McCoys lived on opposite sides of the Tug Fork River, and fought a legendary feud over everything—the Civil War, women, even pigs—for 20 years.

PEEK AT PRISON

Curious about life behind bars? Visit Moundsville and take the State Penitentiary Tour. The prison was closed in 1995, but now serves to give people a true taste of lockup.

LAKE SUPERIOR

SUPERIOR
Manitou Falls
Apostle Islands

MICHIGAN

St. Croix

CAMERON
Pioneer Village Museum

EAU CLAIRE

Chippewa

MINNESOTA

Mississippi

Flambeau

Northern Highland

Timm's Hill

Menominee

WISCONSIN

WAUSAU

Central Plain

Wisconsin

Mississippi River

LA CROSSE
Circus World Museum

BARABOO

Taliesin Home

Wisconsin

House on the Rock

MADISON

Wisconsin State Capitol

Lake Winnebago

APPLETON

Lizard Mound State Park

Wisconsin State Fair

Lambeau Field

Oneida Nation Museum

Green Bay

Door County

GREEN BAY

Fox

MANITOWOC

Wisconsin Maritime Museum

LAKE MICHIGAN

WEST BEND

MILWAUKEE

WEST ALLIS

RACINE

Racine Reef Lighthouse

MICHIGAN

IOWA

ILLINOIS

N W E S

0 60 Miles

QUICK FACTS

State capital: Madison
Largest city: Milwaukee
Total area: 65,498 square miles (169,640 sq km)
Highest point: Timm's Hill in Price County, 1,952 feet (595 m)
Lowest point: 579 feet (176 m) along Lake Michigan

RIDDLES RACES

In 1985, Madison's Libby Riddles became the first woman to win Alaska's famous dogsled race, the Iditarod, which won her a place in the Iditarod Hall of Fame.

THE GIANT "MUSKIE"

Hayward hosts a giant muskellunge, which is half a block long, and four and a half stories high. It's considered the highlight of the National Freshwater Fishing Hall of Fame.

ENAMEL TRANSFORMATION

In 1883, John Michael Kohler of Sheboygan coated a pigs' watering trough with enamel, and realized that he'd just made the Kohler Company's first bathtub. So he sold it!

THE BADGER STATE

Wisconsin is the Badger State. In the 1830s, Wisconsin lead miners lived in hillside caves resembling badger dens, and the miners were known as badgers. The name stuck!

EARTH DAY INITIATOR

Long before it was cool to care about the environment, Senator Gaylord Nelson of Clear Lake lobbied for a national day of awareness. The first Earth Day was celebrated on April 22, 1970.

JUMP FOR JOY!

Bloomer, the "Rope Jump Capital of the World," hosts an annual speed jump rope contest for students in grades one through eight. The finals are held each year in January.

HOUDINI'S HOME

Ehrich Weiss, also known as "The Great Houdini," grew up in Appleton. The "master of mystery," who set the bar for magicians everywhere, is considered the world's best escapologist.

FEROCIOUS FIRE

Though the Great Chicago Fire grabbed all the headlines in 1871, an even more devastating fire ripped through the forests of Peshtigo on the same day, killing thousands.

ELEPHANTS ON PARADE!

Milwaukee's Great Circus Parade strolls for three miles through the town with over 75 vintage circus wagons, hundreds of horses, and yes, lots of elephants.

SUPER BOWL HISTORY

The Green Bay Packers won the first Super Bowl in American history held in Los Angeles in 1967. Coach Vince Lombardi's team slammed the Kansas City Chiefs, 35-10.

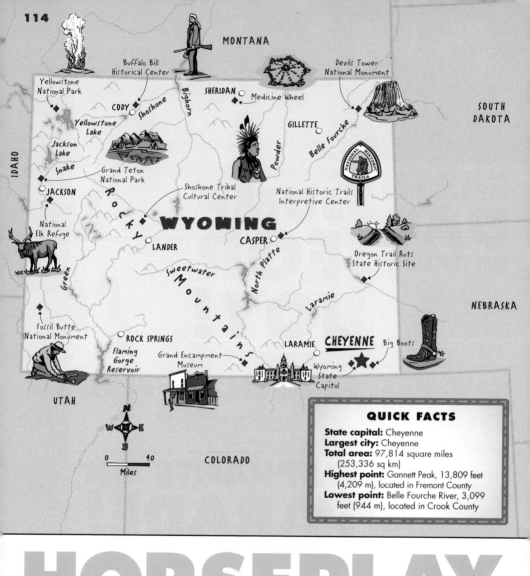

MONTANA

Yellowstone National Park

Buffalo Bill Historical Center

SHERIDAN

Devils Tower National Monument

SOUTH DAKOTA

CODY Shoshone

Bighorn

Medicine Wheel

Yellowstone Lake

GILLETTE

Jackson Lake

Powder

Belle Fourche

Snake

Grand Teton National Park

IDAHO

JACKSON

Shoshone Tribal Cultural Center

WYOMING

National Historic Trails Interpretive Center

National Elk Refuge

Rocky

LANDER

CASPER

Sweetwater

North Platte

Oregon Trail Ruts State Historic Site

Green

Mountains

Laramie

NEBRASKA

Fossil Butte National Monument

ROCK SPRINGS

Flaming Gorge Reservoir

Grand Encampment Museum

LARAMIE

CHEYENNE

Big Boots

Wyoming State Capitol

UTAH

N W E S

0 40
Miles

COLORADO

QUICK FACTS

State capital: Cheyenne
Largest city: Cheyenne
Total area: 97,814 square miles (253,336 sq km)
Highest point: Gannett Peak, 13,809 feet (4,209 m), located in Fremont County
Lowest point: Belle Fourche River, 3,099 feet (944 m), located in Crook County

HORSEPLAY

The bucking bronco on the Wyoming license plate is Steamboat, a legendary horse who refused to be ridden, bucking off the best rodeo riders of the early 20th century.

WYOMING IN SPACE

When the *Voyager* was sent into space in 1977, it contained a photograph of Jackson Hole by the famous photographer Ansel Adams—just in case there is anyone out there.

NO SWIMMING!

Don't ever go swimming in the beautiful blue Morning Glory Pool in Yellowstone National Park. You might dissolve as a result of the pool's high acidity. Ouch!

RODEO BUCKS

In Wyoming, you don't have to be a football player to get an athletic scholarship. The National Intercollegiate Rodeo Association offers scholarships to top rodeo athletes!

BIG BEAR!

Devil's Tower, the national monument featured in *Close Encounters of the Third Kind*, has a striped surface that Sioux legend says was caused by a bear clawing at the sides.

LEGEND OR REALITY?

The jackalope is a beloved creature in Wyoming—to those who believe it exists, anyway. The antlered rabbit is said to be able to run at close to 90 miles per hour. (Hmmm . . .)

PENNEY'S PENNIES

James Cash Penney bought the Golden Rule Store in Kemmerer in 1902, changed the name to JC Penney, and started down the path to riches and success!

CEMENT CAKES!

Nearly 40,000 people come to the free pancake breakfasts during the 10-day rodeo Cheyenne Frontier Days. The demand for pancakes is so great, the batter is sometimes mixed in cement trucks.

AHEAD OF THE GAME

Wyoming women were the first in the nation to be given the right to vote. In fact, they had the right to vote as soon as the Wyoming Territory was formed, in 1869.

DUDE, WHERE'S MY RANCH?

Crossed Sabres Ranch was the first dude ranch in Wyoming. Legend has it that the term "dude" referred to easterners who wanted to vacation on a ranch.

WYOMING

THE COWBOY STATE

Congratulations to the contest winners (listed below) and thanks to all the contributors!

Elizabeth Moreau, AK	Jean Bardwell, MT
Lisa Churchill, AL	LouAnne Krantz, MT
Karen Scott, AL	Holly Pierce, NC
Melisa Rutherford, AR	Cindy Struth, NC
Melissa Wilson, AR	Susan Kempel, ND
Michele Harbour, AZ	Karen Retzlaff, ND
Brandee MacLean, AZ	Paula Ashford, NE
Stephanie Ghinn, CA	Beth Foulks, NE
Shannon Hunsinger, CA	Nancy Polito, NH
Cindi Bryant, CO	Lesley Unger-Mochrie, NH
Diane Webster, CO	Alice DiNizo, NJ
Lisa Plavin, CT	Lynn Hotz, NJ
Susan Ritter, CT	Kathy Barco, NM
Barbara Miller, DC	Marla Layman, NM
Donna Reed, DE	Mary Jo King, NV
Louisa Romaine, DE	Shannon Broderick, NY
Joan Molozaiy, FL	Nancy Williams, NY
Marie Valletta, FL	Mary Gresco, OH
Patricia Tucker, GA	Sharon Touchton, OH
Elaine Walker, GA	Mary Green, OK
Carolyn Kirio, HI	Carolyn Gutierrez, OK
Sandra Ongie, HI	Renee Allen, OR
Karol Dudley, IA	Julianne Brinker, OR
Joy Stoker-Hadow, IA	Barbara Flynn, PA
Lara Alexander, ID	Gail McDonald, PA
Janice Simon, ID	Susan Baxter, RI
Kathy Hempel, IL	Lu Bickley, SC
April Johns, IL	Jan Dandridge, SC
Agnes George, IN	Nancy Allee, TN
Roberta Kobbe, KS	Lynnette Poston, TN
Marcia O'Grady, KS	Shangruti Desai, TX
Prestine Chapman, KY	Peggy Shaw, TX
Suzanne Jameson, LA	Susan Huff, UT
Mia Orgeron, LA	Beverly Stout, UT
Lyn Holian, MA	Genevieve Gallagher, VA
Cathy Rosenstock, MA	Joyce Nelson, VA
Paula Borinsky, MD	Martha Allen, VT
Richard Parker, MD	Cheryl Cox, VT
Jacquie Sewell, MI	Deborah Allen, WA
Patricia Thunell, MI	Kaylene Flanary, WA
Susan Boulka, MN	Anita Folgert, WI
Elena Williams, MN	Ann Salt, WI
Diane Burger, MO	Pamela Mann, WV
Cherie LeMay, MO	Holly Baker, WY
Jackie Jernigan, MS	Mary Wegher, WY

Photographs © 2010: age fotostock/ Stuart Pearce: 15 top left; Alamy Images: 54 (AA World Travel Library), 73 bottom left (David Ball), 43 bottom right (Walter Bibikow/Jon Arnold Images Ltd), 53 top (Dennis Cox), 9 center left, 105 bottom right (Sharon Lowe), cover bottom left background (Mike Perry), 7 bottom left, 55 top (Greg Ryan), 5, 7 top left, 35 bottom right (Don Smetzer); Courtesy of A'Lelia Bundles/ Walker Family Collection: 37 top; AP Images: 47 center left (Robert F. Bukaty), 43 bottom left (James Crisp), 59 top left (Christopher Gannon/Tribune), 13 center (Al Grillo), 65 top right (Brad Horn/Nevada Appeal), 41 bottom right (Dan Loh), 107 bottom (Elaine Thompson), 31 bottom right (USPS), 57 bottom right, 71 center left; Charles Petrocci: 49 top left; Corbis Images: 11 bottom left, 17 bottom right, 21 top, 29 bottom right, 43 center left, 51 bottom left, 53 bottom right, 105 top right (Bettmann), 106 (Gary Braasch), 61 top (William Campbell), 29 bottom left (Jacques M. Chenet), 41 center right, 45 top left (Philip Gould), 71 bottom (Hulton-Deutsch Collection), 65 top left (Dan Lamont), 57 top left (Michael Ochs Archives), 13 top left (David Samuel Robbins), 31 bottom left (Jim Sugar), 87 bottom left (N.C. Wyeth/K.J. Historical); Danita Delimont Stock Photography/Bill Bachmann: 13 bottom; David Franck: back cover, 9 center right, 21 bottom, 33 center, 35 bottom left, 41 top, 73 top left, 91 top, 92, 107 top left; DelmarvaDigital.com/Tim Smith: 25 top left; Dover Motorsports, Inc.: 6 center right, 25 top right; Erik Nygren: 50; Everett Collection, Inc.: 51 center (© Paramount), 91 bottom left (Buena Vista Pictures), 109 bottom right (Joel Jeffries/Comedy Central), 45 bottom right (Warner Bros.); Explore Minnesota Tourism/ Paul Stafford: 55 bottom center; Fotolia: 49 top right (Clarence Alford), 105 top left (Adam Bies), 27 center (W. Doering), 19 bottom right, 25 bottom right (iofoto), 15 bottom left, 88 (JJAVA), 8 top left, 63 center right (Tamara Kulikova), 105 bottom left (James Seidl), 109 center left (Emanuel Zweigel); Getty Images: 113 bottom right (Michael Burr), 93 bottom right (David Corio/Michael Ochs Archives), 81 bottom right, 87 bottom center, 89 bottom right, 99 center (Hulton Archive), 27 bottom right (Streeter Lecka), 13 top right (Joe McNally), 55 bottom left (MGM Studios), 65 bottom left (Mike Nelson/AFP), 6 top left, 11 top left (Bill Pugliano), 65 bottom right (Mark Sandten/Bongarts), 77 bottom right (Jerry Wachter/Sports Imagery); Globe Photos: 6 bottom right, 33 bottom right; Houghton Mifflin Harcourt Publishing Company/Jacket Art © 2005 Francois Roca: 75 bottom right; Idaho Department of Commerce - Division of Tourism Development/Jack Williams: 33 bottom left; Institute for Regional Studies, NDSU Libraries, Fargo: 1, 39 bottom left (Nils C. Jorgenson/rs00816), 79 bottom left (Lee & Co./P66.1); IowaTug Fest/Chuck Creecy: 38; iStockphoto: 56 (Terry J. Alcorn), 27 bottom left (Andrew Ashby), 8 top left, 85 center right (Dariusz Bajak), 6 top left, 16 (BlackJack3D), 47 top (blaneyphoto), 99 top (Ben Conlan), 76 (Christopher Dodge), 69 center right (Mark Evans), 73 top center (Jill Fromer), 49 bottom left (David Gough), 4, 101 top right (Richard Hobson), 4 bottom left, 87 bottom right (Geoffrey Holman), 18 (Home Studio), 89 center (Teresa Hurst), 36, 103 top right (Eric Isselée), 83 top left (Jitalia17), 49 top center (JuniperCreek), 15 top right (Kristin Kanan), 85 bottom right (Elena Korenbaum), 9 bottom left, 113 center (Tommi Laurila), 26 (Marcus Lindstrom), 74 (marco pat), 95 top center right, 51 bottom right (Marek Mnich), 15 bottom right (BreAnn Mueller), 30 left (Skip O'Donnell), 83 top right (P_Wei), 94 (Jon Patton), 83 center (photopalace), 6 bottom left, 31 top (Steven Phraner), 17 top left (PLAINVIEW), 93 bottom left (Lone Elisa Plougmann), 45 center (Jack Puccio), 7 top right, 39 top (ranplett), 59 center (Wesley Richardson), 43 top (Feije Riemersma), 17 center (Suzannah Skelton), 109 bottom left (Eliza Snow), 17 top right (Rob Sylvan), 115 center right (Michael Thompson), 63 top (Ales Veluscek), 12 right (Jonathan Wick), 21 center left (Chris Williams), 57 center (Mark Wragg), 20 left (Ufuk Zivana); Julie Niesen and Terry Gosdin: 11 top right; Courtesy of the Kansas Sampler Foundation: 41 center left; Courtesy of Keeler Tavern Museum: 22; Kobal Collection/Picture Desk/MGM: 81 bottom left; Landov, LLC/Tony Spina/MCT: 53 center; Courtesy of Laura Ingalls Wilder Historic Home and Museum: 95 bottom left; Lebrecht Music Collection/Joe Bangay: 52; Library of Congress: 57 bottom left (Clifford Kennedy Berryman), 91 bottom right (Brady's National Portrait Gallery), 75 bottom left (Currier & Ives), 97 top left (N. Currier/ Currier & Ives), 63 center left (Heyn & Matzen), 70 left (Dorothea Lange/Farm Security Administration-Office of War Information Photograph Collection), 34 (Waterman Co. - Chicago, Ill.), 11 bottom center; NASA: 33 top; National Baseball Hall of Fame Library, Cooperstown, NY: 47 center right; National Park Service: 93 top left (Fort Sumter National Monument), 61 center right (Yellowstone National Park), 104; NEWSCOM/SHNS/Courtesy of Levi Coffin House Association: 37 center left; North Dakota Buffalo Foundation/National Buffalo Museum: 79 top; North Dakota Tourism Department: 79 center right (Pat Hertz), 79 bottom left (Barbara Stitzer), 78 (Bruce Wendt); Oregon State University/ P003:5265: 85 center left; Courtesy of philotfarnsworth.com: 33 bottom center; Photo Researchers, NY/BSIP: 103 top left; Photodisc, Inc.: 7 center, 53 bottom left, 71 center right; Photoshot/David Iushewitz/ Bruce Coleman Inc.: 112; Courtesy of President's Park: 95 top right; Retna Ltd./ Adam Cordell/TSPL/Camera Press: 81 top left; Reuters/Lucy Pemoni: 30 right; RoadsideAmerica.com/Kirby, Smith and Wilkins: 37 bottom left; 68; Courtesy of the Runestone Museum: 55 bottom right; ShutterStock, Inc.: 42 (aaaah), 57 top right (akva), 28 bottom right (Alexphoto), 75 center (almagami), 98 (Aaron Amat), 83 bottom (Nagy-Bagoly Arpad), 19 bottom left (Teresa Azevedo), 113 top (Dan Bannister), 91 center (Laurie Barr), 101 bottom right (BenC), 37 bottom right (Nadezhda Bolotina), 62 (Chad Bontrager), 27 top (Pavel Bortel), cover top right (Joy Brown), 17 bottom left (Katrina Brown), 111 top left (Sascha Bukard), 20 right (George Burba), 107 top right (Norman Chan), 77 top left (Willee Cole), 59 bottom (dalereardon), 60 (Zacarias Pereira de Mata), 95 bottom right (Peder Digre), 115 center left (Qing Ding), 40 (Dr_Flash), 115 top right (Elemental Imaging), 101 top left (Daryl Faust), 111 top right (Stephen Finn), 96 (Mike Flippo), 8 center left, 75 top left (Kellie L. Folkerts), 21 center right (Jeffrey M. Frank), 86 (Alan Freed), 111 bottom (K. Geijer), 35 bottom center (Reiulf Gronnevik), 61 bottom (Sirko Hartmann), 23 top right (Chris Harvey), 8 center, 77 bottom left (J. Helgason), 9 bottom right, 109 top (Douglas R. Hess), 101 bottom left (iofoto), 12 left (Alexander Ishchenko), cover top left, 14, 63 bottom (Eric Isselée), 8 top right, 69 bottom (joroma), 109 center right (Joseph), 51 top (JustASC), 10 (Kelpfish), 97 top right (KennStilger47), 69 top (Milan Kryl), 7 center left, 47 center (Morgan Lane Library), cover center, 6 center left, 19 top left, 115 bottom right (Morgan Lane Photography), 81 center (Muriel Lasure), 89 bottom right (RJ Lerich), 77 center (Robyn Mackenzie), 9 top right, 97 bottom right (Maxx-Studio), 47 bottom (Mazzzur), 72 (Mike McDonald), 69 center left (MdN), 70 left (Terence Mendoza), 64 (Steven Newton), 48 (Heath Oldham), 73 top right (Emin Ozkan), 19 top right (Marc Pagani Photography), 8 center right, 81 top right (Pakmor), 75 top right (pandapaw), 43 center right (Kirsty Pargeter), 7 bottom left, 58 (Thomas M. Perkins), 45 bottom left (Leigh Prather), 90 (Rambleon), 100 (Elena Ray), 11 bottom right (Karen Roach), 113 bottom left (Willie Rossin), cover bottom left foreground (Julian Rovagnati), 89 top (R. Gino Santa Maria), 99 bottom (Brandon Seidel), 4 bottom right, 8 bottom left, 87 top (Andrea Skjold), 102 (Lori Sparkia), cover bottom right (Dick Stada), 79 bottom right (Tatjana Strelkova), 19 top center (Christophe Testi), 115 bottom left (Cory Thoman), 61 center left (Trinacria Photo), 41 bottom left (Vinicius Tupinamba), 29 top, 37 center right, 59 top center (Joao Virissimo), 28 (Valentyn Volkov), 59 top center (David Watkins), 9 top left, 93 top right (Jamie Wilson); Courtesy of Smithsonian's National Zoo: 108; Steve Greer Photography: 71 top; Steve Pope Photography: 39 bottom right; StockFood, Inc./TH Foto: 44; Tekla Photography: 103 bottom; The Field Museum, Chicago, IL./ John Weinstein/GEO86197c/Sculpture by Brian Cooley: 35 top; The Granger Collection, New York: 23 top left (Barnum & Bailey), 25 bottom left, 45 top right, 59 top right; Courtesy of the The Peabody Memphis: 97 bottom left; Courtesy of the University of Connecticut, Division of Athletics: 23 bottom; University of Oregon Museum of Natural and Cultural History/Lack Liu: 85 bottom left; US Mint: 23 top center; Vector-Images.com: 69 center, 73 bottom right, 82, 85 top; Courtesy of West Virginia University: 110; William P. Gottlieb: 49 bottom right.